THE NEW DEAL
AND THE GREAT
DEPRESSION IN
AMERICAN HISTORY

Other titles *in American History*

IN
AMERICAN
HISTORY

THE NEW DEAL AND THE GREAT DEPRESSION IN AMERICAN HISTORY

Lisa A. Wroble

Enslow Publishers, Inc.

40 Industrial Road   PO Box 38
Box 398   Aldershot
Berkeley Heights, NJ 07922   Hants GU12 6BP
USA   UK

http://www.enslow.com

To Mom and Dad, and all who endured the Great Depression,
learning to find happiness
"in the joy of achievement, in the thrill of creative effort."

Library of Congress Cataloging-in-Publication Data

Wroble, Lisa A.
　　The New Deal and the Great Depression in American history / Lisa A.
Wroble.
　　　　p. cm. — (In American history)
　　Includes bibliographical references (p.) and index.
　　Summary: Examines the history of the Great Depression and details the
New Deal programs designed to bring relief to the American people and the
economy, highlighting the role of President Franklin Roosevelt and showing
the impact of his policies on ordinary poeple.
　　ISBN 0-7660-1421-5
　　1. United States—History—1933-1945—Juvenile literature. 2. New
Deal, 1933-1939—Juvenile literature. 3. Depressions—1929—United
States—Juvenile literature. 4. Roosevelt, Franklin D. (Franklin Delano),
1882-1945—Juvenile literature. 5. United States—Economic conditions—
1918-1945—Juvenile literature. [1. United States—History—1933-1945.
2. New Deal, 1933-1939. 3. Depressions—1929. 4. Roosevelt, Franklin D.
(Franklin Delano), 1882-1945. 5. United States—Economic conditions—
1918-1945.] I. Title. II. Series.
E806 .W785 2002
973.917—dc21

　　　　　　　　　　　　　　　　　　　　　　　　　　　　2001007432

Printed in the United States of America

10 9 8 7 6 5 4 3 2 1

To Our Readers:
We have done our best to make sure all Internet addresses in this book were
active and appropriate when we went to press. However, the author and the
publisher have no control over and assume no liability for the material available
on those Internet sites or on other Web sites they may link to. Any comments or
suggestions can be sent by e-mail to comments@enslow.com or to the address
on the back cover.

Illustration Credits: Courtesy of the Franklin D. Roosevelt Library, Hyde Park,
New York, pp. 18, 34, 61, 63, 88; Enslow Publishers, Inc., p. 82; National
Archives and Records Administration, pp. 22, 24, 25, 28, 35, 45, 49, 64, 98,
100, 102, 104, 107; Reproduced from the Collections of the Library of
Congress, pp. 30, 69, 85, 89.

Cover Illustration: Courtesy of the Franklin D. Roosevelt Library, Hyde Park,
New York; National Archives and Records Administration; Reproduced from the
Collections of the Library of Congress.

★ CONTENTS ★

THE FORGOTTEN MAN

We are the first nation in the history of the world to go to the poor-house in an automobile.[1]

—Will Rogers, actor and humorist, 1931

The years 1935 and 1936 were important for New Deal programs. The New Deal was launched by President Franklin D. Roosevelt in 1933 to deal with the problems of the Great Depression. The Great Depression was an historic period of worldwide economic decline. Americans worked hard. New agencies, like the Works Progress Administration (WPA), were created under the New Deal. The United States was slowly trying to pull itself out of the Depression. Then unemployment started to inch upward, reaching some of the worst levels of the Depression. Middle-class men found themselves unemployed. Mr. Donner (full name unavailable) owned a printing business in Chicago. He struggled to keep it open during the early years of the Depression. He eventually lost all his money and had to live with his wife's parents in Dubuque, Iowa.

"He thinks now that he held on too long, but he had no way of knowing the depression would last so long, and that in the end he would save nothing from his business," an interviewer for a WPA research study recorded.[2]

In an effort to remain off relief, Mr. Donner took a WPA job. He wore overalls daily for his work as a laborer. Mrs. Donner (full name unavailable) admitted she cried after her husband left for work. She did not like seeing him reduced to common labor after owning his own business. She said, "He had never had a pair of overalls, not even when he was a little boy."[3]

The Donners were not alone. Letters poured into the White House asking the president, first lady, and leaders of New Deal programs for help. The WPA added federal programs to employ writers, actors, musicians, and artists in August 1935.[4] The National Youth Administration was formed to provide student work programs for people high school aged and older.[5] With these added programs, more people should have been employed. But they did not feel a lull in the poverty of the Depression. Some thought the problems of the forgotten man—the common man—were due to opposition to New Deal programs.

Some industry and political leaders claimed that after years of federal help, the common man was becoming lazy. They felt he was looking for relief rather than trying to help himself.[6] Donner had heard these stories. He had seen some of these workers himself. "Of course," Donner said, "there are a few loafers on WPA projects; but there are also a few loafers on jobs in private industry."[7]

Donner was not bitter about his circumstances. He hoped to stop working for the WPA soon. He looked to a day when he might run his own business again.[8] Despite some leaders' views, Donner believed that without some New Deal programs the country would surely have undergone a violent overthrow of the government—as was occurring in Europe and Asia.[9]

Many people believed these projects were busywork handed out to people to ease their pride in accepting welfare (monetary aid). Some of the workers themselves even thought the projects were not absolutely necessary. These public works projects may not have been entirely necessary, but they benefitted the country. While the Depression would end someday, the improved cities, paved roads, parks, buildings, and works of art created by these New Deal programs would be enjoyed by future generations.

2

SHATTERED PROSPERITY

The 1920s were a time of prosperity often called the Roaring Twenties. A boom in industry after World War I created jobs. People had money to spend. With an increase in assembly-line manufacturing the middle class grew. Before the war, people fell into two categories—the rich upper class and the poor lower class, mostly farmers and laborers. For centuries, merchants created a small middle class between these two groups. But as manufacturing grew, poor people moved from rural areas to work in cities. Many filled jobs in industry and worked their way up to the middle class.

Consuming Fun

The economy soared. Americans learned to spend their money as quickly as they made it. Automaker Henry Ford once said, "Mass production requires mass consumption."[2] During the 1920s, America became a consumer culture. People enjoyed life. They had good jobs and money to spend. They balanced the fruits of their labor with social outings, where they could show off recent purchases, such as automobiles.

The automobile best symbolized the emerging tendency to spend money during the 1920s. It became a focal point in the American way of life. In 1919, there were 6 million cars on the United States roads. By 1929, as the Roaring Twenties came to a close, there were 23 million. "The automobile industry exploited Americans' enormous appetite not just for transportation but for style," wrote Vincent Virga and Alan Brinkley in *Eyes of the Nation*.[3]

Young people especially joined the roar of fun during the 1920s. Americans demonstrated their vitality with late-night dances, movies, musicals, and various campus antics. Teenagers also invented contests to fill their free time. Dance marathons were popular. Couples competed with each other to see who could dance continuously for the longest time. These dances often lasted twenty-four hours or longer. Setting records—for the longest time sitting atop telephone poles, or for swallowing goldfish—was fashionable. Free time was no longer only a privilege of the upper class. The emerging middle class in America had raised its expectations for not only better jobs and improved living standards, but for ways to spend money. The high prosperity and clamor of fun celebrated by the Roaring Twenties provided plenty of opportunity.

Not everyone shared in the wealth—of money or time—however. "The fruits of this growth were, to be sure, unevenly shared," according to Virga and Brinkley,

> Most farmers, workers, and minorities realized only small gains, or none at all, despite the boom—a problem that would gradually undermine the economy and help bring it crashing down. But for members of the middle class, and for many others, the 1920s expanded their incomes and hence greatly increased purchasing power.[4]

The Lure of Wall Street

One opportunity available for spending newly gained wealth brought with it the lure of Wall Street. Wall Street was the banking district in New York City where the New York Stock Exchange (NYSE) was housed. The NYSE was the largest and most active stock market in the country. To the average American, Wall Street equaled financial power. That power was available only to the upper class who could afford to invest their money, then forget about it for a while. Purchasing stocks is actually buying a piece of a company—called a share—then sharing in that company's profits or losses. Each investor receives a certificate showing the shares held, or the percentage owned, in a company. As company profits rise, stock values rise.

The American economy was healthy prior to the 1920s. After World War I ended in 1918, American businesses grew and many traded with European countries trying to rebuild after the war. Following a recession, or slowdown in business, between 1920 and 1922, the American economy was once again healthy. American banks made private loans to help finance the reconstruction in war-torn countries. This business helped stock prices climb higher. As Europe recovered from the destruction of World War I, the economy grew stronger and prices rose.

For the average American the share prices were out of reach. But a new method for purchasing shares brought this investing power to more Americans than ever before. Investors bought shares of stock by borrowing money from their brokers. This allowed the growing middle class to invest money in the stock market.

A Margin of Power

This new method of paying for shares of stock led to an increase in stock purchases. It was called "buying on margin," which meant the broker paid for part of the share. When the shares were sold, the broker would be paid back. If the investor and the broker handled the purchase and sale properly, there would be plenty of profit made to cover the "margin loan" as well as plenty left for reinvestment or more spending.

Not only average people invested this way. Businesses, large and small, invested in the stock market by buying on margin. Buying on margin allowed investors to make investments with values five or ten times greater than they would have been able to afford without the loan.[5] Even banks invested their holdings— the money deposited by customers—in the stock market.

"Today, if you want to buy $100 worth of stock, you have to put up $80 and the broker will put up $20. In those days," according to business owner Arthur Robertson, "you could put up $8 or $10. . . . There were not the controls you have today."[6]

New ways to join this frenzied, or wild, focus on the stock market developed. One type was a pool. A group of investors would buy and sell a certain stock so the flurry of activity attracted inexperienced investors. As more stocks were sold, the price rose. When they reached a profitable level, the group of investors in the pool sold all their shares at top price. This made the value of the stock fall quickly. Pooling was not illegal or secret.

President Herbert Hoover, along with other government officials, economists, and bankers, realized the heavy speculation, or buying on margin, needed to slow down. The Federal Reserve Board, which controlled the funds available to banks in the United States, could have limited the money available for stock market loans. However, Hoover was concerned that such a limit would send warnings of danger and "might cause the very collapse he wanted to prevent."[7]

It was not only speculation buying that was a growing concern. Inexperienced investors were outwitted by investment trusts and holding companies. An investment trust was a corporation that bought stocks of other companies. Among the public utilities, like electric power companies, the corporation that bought the stocks was called a holding company. The trusts and holding companies were often piled. That is, new trusts or holding companies were created to purchase shares from those trusts above them in the pile. All the companies sold shares to the public. To the innocent investor this meant that shares in Company C were only one third of the shares purchased by the original (Company A) trust or holding company. A stock certificate—and the prices on the stock market— would make it seem that the stock value was higher than it really was. Those who set up the investment, not the other investors, profited the most.

All of this added up to increased activity on the stock market. There was so much investing that stock prices soon rose to their highest rates ever. The market could not sustain this growth, however. In September 1929, prices began to drop. Regular investors in the stock market knew that normal business practice resulted in prices going up and down. But to those middle-class Americans who had invested more than they could afford, falling prices meant they might not be able to cover their loans. Many people panicked and sold their stocks. Brokers panicked, too, and put out "margin calls" asking for loans to be paid back. This rapid selling caused prices to fall even more.

One historian described the scenario on Wall Street during October 1929:

> These investors counted on rising prices to cover their loans when they sold stock. It was a bad bet: Prices slipped in early October. Brokers sent margin calls to their clients demanding payment of their loans. Many investors were forced to sell some or all of their stock because they didn't have the cash to repay their brokers.

Such sales pushed prices even lower, causing still more losses and provoking new waves of margin calls. By the week of October 22 selling had reached panic pitch.[8]

The panicked selling was at first met with frenzied buying at low rates by experts in the stock market game. As worried investors made the agonizing decision[9] whether to sell or hold out for prices to rise again, the churning market stopped their hopes of prosperity.[10] In brokers' offices across the country, the same scene played out again and again. Rookie traders made the decision to sell before they lost even more, only to watch the market struggle a few points higher. This increase would have at least covered their margin loan. "Every move was wrong, in those days. The market seemed like an insensate [foolish and brutal] thing that was wreaking a wild and pitiless revenge upon those who had thought to master it," wrote Elliott V. Bell, a reporter for the *New York Times*, in 1929.[11]

Prices plummeted steadily between October 22 and October 29. Attempting to reverse the impending crash, the heads of six banks agreed to pool money in the hopes of maintaining a "'cushion' of buying power"[12] under the falling market. Each banker pledged $40 million to the pool. Other financial institutions sent unsolicited offers of funds to add to the pool. The total reserves this meeting produced—$340 million—was inadequate.[13] On October 29, 1929, market share values bottomed-out, or reached zero profit. The stock market had crashed.

According to Bell,

It [the crash] came with a speed and ferocity that left men dazed. The bottom simply fell out of the market. From all over the country a torrent of selling orders poured onto the floor of the stock exchange and there were no buying orders to meet it. Quotations of representative active issues, like steel [U.S. Steel], telephone [AT&T], and Anaconda, began to fall two, three, five, and even ten points between sales.[14]

In the Dust of the Crash

"In the strange way that news of a disaster spreads, the word of the market collapse flashed through the city. By noon great crowds had gathered at the corner of Broad and Wall Streets . . . traffic was pushed from the streets of the financial district by the crush," reported Bell.[15]

Overnight, the "roar" of the 1920s faded. Millions of people lost everything. Even those who never invested in the stock market were affected because banks had also invested their holdings in the stock market. When the banks where people held accounts folded, millions more lost every dime they had ever earned.

Even children were feeling the effects of the crash. Clancy Strock, who was nine years old when the Depression hit, said, "I lost my life savings. It amounted to something on the order of $8 and change, as best I can remember. But it was pretty serious to me then. Fact was, the bank had closed and I was wiped out." Banks were places with guards and vaults where Strock felt "insofar as I knew, my $8 was under safekeeping. I was wrong. And now I was ruined."[16]

With no insurance on deposits, people rushed to withdraw their money from banks after the stock market crash.

The business world knew that the economy had its ups and downs. As the dust cleared after the crash, most industry leaders waited for the economy to level itself out. Hoover asked business and industry leaders to project a sense of hope. He asked them to maintain wage levels and not cut their workforces. He also asked them to continue investing in their own industries as well as others. Though they agreed with the president, "most paid little more than lip service to the promises they had made to Hoover."[17]

Small businesses especially struggled. Once-prosperous store owners now found themselves in serious financial trouble. To compensate they let employees go. By the end of 1929, 1.4 million people were unemployed, out of a total labor force of 48 million workers.[18]

"Overcome with despair, many Americans reluctantly discarded their deeply held belief in rugged individualism and self-reliance and turned finally to the federal government as a last resort. And in 1929 few Americans seemed better suited to deal with such widespread calamity than the newly elected president, Herbert Hoover," wrote historian Roger Biles.[19]

Americans felt Hoover was the man for this difficult job. After all, as President Woodrow Wilson's food administrator during World War I, he had managed to feed nearly 10 million people in the warring nations of Europe. When the United States entered the war, the term "Hooverize" became a household word for doing without meat one day or wheat on another day. It was all part of his role as head of the United States Food Administration. He also headed the American Relief Administration, which distributed food and clothing to more than 30 million people on the war-torn continent of Europe.[20]

The American people wondered: Could President Hoover do something to feed and clothe the American victims of the Great Depression?

DOWN AND OUT

While the American people waited for help, Hoover waited for the banking crisis to end. His background as a mining engineer and businessman lent itself to watching numbers and finances. He, as well as other businessmen, had seen the unsteady rise and fall of profit. He believed the economy would correct itself—given time and carefully watched spending. He and his advisors thought that if Americans could be patient and ride out this slump, the economy would level out.

Hoover cut income tax. He also urged volunteerism—people helping those in their own communities. Soup kitchens run by churches, the Red Cross, and other aid societies, grew in number. The Reconstruction Finance Corporation (RFC) was created to help banks and other companies avoid bankruptcy. Hoover also sponsored conservation and public works projects, which created jobs. One well-known project was the Boulder Dam, later renamed the Hoover Dam. Despite these efforts, more and more people lost their homes and jobs.

Men wandered the cities looking for jobs. Families turned to the long lines of the local soup kitchens for food. Families were split apart as husbands and older sons left home. They hopped trains to neighboring towns. They hoped to find work and money to send home.

Harvesting jobs were supposed to be plentiful in the West. Millions of Americans escaped to California, loading their cars with all their belongings. If they were unable to find work, they settled in temporary homes made out of scrap materials. These shantytowns became permanent homes to the down-and-out.

Hoboes and Hoovervilles

Of the millions of penniless wanderers in the country, an estimated two hundred thousand were children. Some were with their families or one parent. Many were alone, fending for themselves. Hunger drove them to look for food in the trash. "There is not a garbage dump in Chicago which is not diligently haunted by the hungry," literary critic Edmund Wilson observed.[2]

Many American people wondered if President Hoover was content allowing people to live in shacks built from trash. Those who were busy trying to survive did not notice the light burning in the president's office long into the night. Many did not

Thin soup, served by the many charities, was the only food millions could get all day. This line at a kitchen in Chicago, Illinois, leads to both bread and soup.

know the president had asked Congress to authorize the RFC to loan $300 million to state and local governments to provide for the needy. Still, Hoover was unable to stem the tide of despair that flowed over the nation.

"[President] Hoover, as a man, took a good deal of this blame personally upon himself," recalled David Kennedy, who was working for the Federal Reserve Board in the 1930s. "It was unjustifiable."[3]

The Great Depression continued to gain a tighter grip on the nation. More people were without jobs and homes. Viewing the shantytowns as a disgrace, the press referred to them as "Hoovervilles."

Phrases meant to mock the president lasted throughout the Depression. Empty, turned-out pockets were called "Hoover flags." Newspapers became known as "Hoover blankets" because hoboes (wandering homeless people) used them to cover themselves as they slept in alleys. When gasoline became too costly, farmers used mules to pull their automobiles and called them "Hoovercarts."[4]

The drifters were not the only ones suffering in the aftermath of the stock market crash. Most industries ran at less than half capacity. Approximately a third of the work force was unemployed by 1933, though this number varied throughout the Depression.[5] In a *U.S. News & World Report* article entitled "1933: The Rise of the Common Man," historian Lewis Lord wrote: "Despair ruled the land. People slept in sewer pipes in Oakland and hunted food in garbage dumps in Chicago. When a puny child in Appalachia complained of being hungry, her teacher told her to go home and eat. 'I can't,' the girl replied. 'It's my sister's turn to eat.'"[6]

President Hoover was quoted as saying, "No one has starved . . . hoboes, for example, are better fed than they have ever been."[7] His reputation continued to decline. A crushing blow came in an incident with World War I veterans. These veterans were entitled to an army bonus to be paid to them in 1945. A group of them, called the Bonus Expeditionary Force, traveled to Washington, D.C., in June 1932 to request early payment. They

During World War I, Herbert Hoover served as President Wilson's food administrator. This poster outlines the praised plan for "Hooverizing," or rotating foods eaten from day to day in order to conserve during wartime. During the Depression, the more negative term "Hoovervilles" became commonplace.

needed the money now—thirteen years was too long to wait. President Hoover declared that charities and local governments—not the federal government—should provide for bankrupt Americans.[8]

Clash on Capitol Hill

Traveling from as far as Oregon, members of the Bonus Expeditionary Force (BEF) brought their ragged families and camped out in Washington, D.C. When the Bonus Bill did not pass the Senate vote, President Hoover feared a riot. Instead, the BEF sang *America* on the steps of Congress and quietly left. Because many of them had nowhere else to go, they remained in their camps. Shantytowns of tar-paper shacks dotted Capitol Hill.

Hoover held his stance. Charity from the federal government was not the answer. He did not feel the federal government had the right to interfere. Charity should come from neighbors or from local and state governments. His Quaker religion had taught him a strong work ethic and service to others. He was convinced people needed to help one another, rather than rely on government aid.[9] He ordered the veterans confined to their camps by police, with the aid of the U.S. Army if necessary.

General Douglas MacArthur, U.S. Army chief of staff, disregarded the president's orders to just confine

Camp Marks, the largest of the Bonus Expeditionary Force's camps in Washington, D.C., is engulfed in flames against the distant image of the Capitol building.

the veterans. He organized removal of the BEF members with his aide, Major Dwight D. Eisenhower. Escorted by tanks, General MacArthur led infantry and cavalry regiments to the edge of the largest camp. Cavalrymen spanned the lot, driving spectators back on the sidewalks. With bayonets fixed, the infantrymen started across the lot. "The soldiers stepped back, pulled teargas bombs from their belts, and hurled them into the midst of the mob. Some of the veterans grabbed the bombs and threw them back at the infantry," wrote Lee McCardell, reporter for the *Baltimore Sun*.[10]

A breeze blew the gas into the faces of the soldiers and the spectators across the street. Eyes watering, the infantrymen managed to torch the camp. The tar-paper shacks were quickly engulfed in flames.[11]

Members of the BEF tried to save at least a few of their belongings before the blaze drove them away. The wind changed direction again sending smoke into the faces of the veterans. For many of the BEF, all that they owned was in the flaming camp. They now truly had nothing. "The casualties included more than one hundred injured veterans and one dead infant," according to Biles.[12]

The blaze from Capitol Hill lit up the sky. It was a message to poor Americans that they would not get help from the nation's leaders. Americans were shocked by the ordeal of the "Bonus Army." It helped many start to believe that a new president was essential for the future of America.[13]

I decline to accept present conditions as inevitable or beyond control.[1]

—Franklin Delano Roosevelt,
Campaign Speech in Boston,
October 31, 1932

CAMPAIGNING A NEW DEAL

Many people wanted Hoover out of office. Franklin D. Roosevelt, the governor of New York, ran for president in 1932 on the Democratic ticket. He had ideas to pull the United States out of its economic slump. In fact, he had already put some of these ideas to work in New York. The rest of the country was ready for the same changes.

When the Depression first hit, Roosevelt thought—as President Hoover did—that patience would see the economy straighten itself out. But as months passed, Roosevelt knew action was necessary. He created ways to help the citizens of New York. He set up a welfare system for the unemployed and gained tax relief for farmers. He also established an old-age pension—a regular payment to those retired from work—and created a conservation and reforestation program. By 1932, he knew similar efforts were needed nationwide. The government, he felt, must

Franklin D. Roosevelt

help the economy by offering assistance. This plan would come to be called the New Deal.

Facing the Issues

During the presidential election of 1932, *Business Week* magazine reported the unemployment rate at 31 percent. Nearly half of all manufacturing had ceased, leaving unemployment in this industry at 46 percent. Steel plants operated at only 12 percent of capacity and coal mines dropped to 30 percent of full operation. While unemployed workers in these industries were reduced to standing in breadlines for their meals, farmers had worse problems because of the Depression.[2]

"The gross national product [value of goods and services produced by a nation] fell by 25 percent from $104 billion in 1929 to $76 billion in 1932. Agricultural prices fell 61 percent from 1929 to 1933, and net farm income decreased from $13 billion to $5.5 billion," wrote historian Roger Biles.[3]

Banks foreclosed—or seized property when mortgages went unpaid—on one third of the farms in the United States. In 1932, for example, 60 percent of North Dakota farms were auctioned, along with their equipment and furniture, so banks could recover lost mortgages and back taxes. During a single day in 1932, officials auctioned off one fourth of rural Mississippi.[4] The former farmers were left with only a few clothes, personal items, and their families. Most had nowhere to go. They watched helplessly as their homes and possessions were sold to the highest bidder.

An auctioneer tries to sell a pitchfork at a farm foreclosure in Tenstrike, Minnesota. Bids at these auctions started at "one penny," so the previous owner could try to buy back some of his or her belongings.

Farmers banded together the only way they could. They traveled to the auctions of friends and neighbors, bidding a penny for each item auctioned. The point of so-called "penny auctions" was to keep the prices low in hopes that their neighbors could buy back their belongings. It also made it difficult for the auction officials to raise funds. Penny auctions were meant to keep the banking system from seizing so much farm property when the nation was in need of the food the farms produced.

Breaking with Tradition

The Democratic party was split in support of Roosevelt or Al Smith. The party's conservative leaders, together with financiers such as John Raskob, a DuPont executive, were opposed to Roosevelt. They favored Al Smith. The conservatives thought Roosevelt's view of government aid as a social duty was dangerously radical.[5] "His many speeches on behalf of the 'forgotten man' clearly cast him as the party's liberal candidate," wrote Roger Biles.[6]

Each political party has a convention where it nominates its candidate for president. Nomination for a presidential candidate required two thirds of the convention's vote. At the 1932 convention of the Democratic party, a "Stop Roosevelt" coalition was able to deny Roosevelt victory through three ballots. In the fourth ballot, Speaker of the House John Nance Garner switched his vote, giving Roosevelt the nomination as the Democratic party's candidate.

Normally, the nominee waited to be informed by a committee. In a history-making move, however, Roosevelt flew from Albany, New York, to Chicago, Illinois, to address the convention delegates in person. He hoped it would show the country, and the Democratic party, that his polio—a crippling disease— would not slow him down. This was the first campaign trip any presidential candidate in history made by plane. It took nine hours for Roosevelt to reach the Democratic convention.

His acceptance speech pledged a "new deal" for the American people. Roosevelt urged his fellow Democrats to help him battle the Great Depression and "restore America to its greatness." He used the phrase "new deal," which became a term that bounced around news reports and political discussions. Americans waited patiently to learn exactly what it meant. His vague speeches did not detail his "new

SOURCE DOCUMENT

I PLEDGE YOU, I PLEDGE MYSELF, TO A NEW DEAL FOR THE AMERICAN PEOPLE. LET US ALL HERE ASSEMBLED CONSTITUTE OURSELVES PROPHETS OF A NEW ORDER OF COMPETENCE AND OF COURAGE. THIS IS MORE THAN A POLITICAL CAMPAIGN; IT IS A CALL TO ARMS. GIVE ME YOUR HELP, NOT TO WIN VOTES ALONE, BUT TO WIN THIS CRUSADE TO RESTORE AMERICA TO ITS OWN PEOPLE.[7]

Franklin D. Roosevelt accepted the presidential nomination in 1932 with these words.

deal" but they did show confidence for a better future.[8]

The American people seemed to cling to Roosevelt's confidence and hope for improvement. They did not seem to notice that his plans for pulling the nation out of the Depression held many contradictions. He called for a balanced budget, a five-day work week, and a 25 percent reduction in federal spending. However, he pushed for establishing unemployment insurance and social security and for building public works, all of which would require more federal spending.

In a campaign speech in Boston, Massachusetts, in October 1932, Roosevelt outlined a three-point program for solving the problems of the unemployed. His first point was that no one in the nation should be permitted to starve. The federal government had to step in if this burden became too great for an individual state. His second point stated that the federal government needed to provide temporary work. His third point would help carry this out. It stated that the federal government should speed up the construction of public works. Due to his use of the phrase in earlier speeches, "the New Deal" became the name for Roosevelt's three-point plan. Many projects already approved by Congress and President Hoover were not slated to begin until summer of 1933 or later.[9]

Roosevelt won the election in a landslide victory, taking 57.4 percent of the popular vote, compared to Hoover's 39.7 percent. Of the forty-eight states in 1932, Hoover only managed to carry the states of Pennsylvania, Vermont, Connecticut, New Hampshire, and Maine.[10] Roosevelt won 472 of the 531 electoral votes. Each state has a certain number of electoral votes based on its population. If a candidate wins a state's popular vote, he then wins its electoral votes. Democrats also captured control of both houses of Congress. In the Senate, 59 of the 95 senators (Florida had only one senator at the time) were Democrats. In the House of Representatives 313 of 430 congressmen were Democrats.[11]

Waiting for Rescue

During the four-month wait between the November election and the March inauguration, the economy continued to slump. Hoover tried to get Roosevelt to endorse his administration's policies during his final days in office. The president-elect resisted. Roosevelt felt this would cause him to share responsibility for

These children, covered with dirt and sores, sit on the porch of a rehabilitation clinic in Arkansas. Early in the Depression, the unemployed and homeless were given a place to stay, food, and aid in finding jobs.

the outgoing administration at worst, and limit his own administration's choices for recovery at the very least.[12] On New Year's Day, 1933, former President Calvin Coolidge made this observation: "In other periods of [economic] depression there has always been hope, but as I look about, I now see nothing to give ground for hope—nothing of man."[13]

In early 1933, people panicked and many banks closed their doors. When William Comstock, governor of Michigan, declared a "bank holiday" on February 14, 1933, 550 banks in the state closed. Other states followed suit. By inauguration day on March 4, 1933, all but one of the forty-eight states had suspended banking. A total of 5,000 banks nationwide, holding combined deposits of $3.4 billion dollars, closed their

A boy on relief in San Leandro, California, carries home a sack stuffed with surplus food.

doors.[14] People were scared. The foundations of the American economy seemed to be buckling.

President Roosevelt was faced with a banking collapse and the highest unemployment rate since the stock market crashed in 1929. Three years and five months after the crash, 11.9 million people, or one in four workers, were without jobs. Roosevelt had a huge task ahead if he planned to follow through on his campaign promise of a New Deal. After his inauguration and speech, which was the first ever broadcast over radio, the American people felt hopeful.

The new president discussed the truth with his fellow Americans frankly and boldly. "So, first of all, let me assert my firm belief that the only thing we have to fear is fear itself—nameless, unreasoning, unjustified terror which paralyzes needed efforts to convert retreat into advance."[15] He spoke of treating the Depression as if it were a national emergency. If this failed, he pledged to use his executive power to "wage a war against the emergency," as if the United States "were in fact invaded by a foreign foe."[16]

The only way to have a friend is to be one.[1]

—Ralph Waldo Emerson, American poet

THE GREAT COMMUNICATOR

Franklin Delano Roosevelt had been involved in Democratic politics for almost a generation. A distant cousin of former President Theodore Roosevelt, Franklin Roosevelt was sixteen years old when he watched his cousin sworn in as governor of New York. Franklin wanted to follow in his cousin's footsteps. It was a likely dream, since he grew up with all the privileges common to New York's upper class.

The Roosevelts had firm roots in the beginnings of the nation. Franklin was proud of the fact that his great-great-grandfather Isaac Roosevelt was among those defying British rule. In 1788, Isaac was involved in the state constitutional convention, held in Poughkeepsie, New York. He cast his vote with the Federalists to ratify the Constitution of the United States.[2] On his mother's side (the Delanos), Franklin traced his heritage to Philippe de la Noye, who arrived with the second shipload of settlers at Plymouth Colony in 1621.[3]

Franklin's understanding of America stemmed from these facts and from the estate where he was raised. He knew he would someday inherit Springwood, which occupied hundreds of acres along the Hudson River south of Hyde Park, New York.

Like other privileged children, Franklin did not attend public school. His mother taught him to read and write before the age of six. Tutors were hired to teach him history, science, geography, arithmetic, and foreign languages, such as Latin, French, and German. He also learned to ride horses, swim, play tennis, play the piano, and dance. When his family took trips in the United States, they traveled in a private railroad car. Franklin often visited Europe with his parents, traveling first-class on the long sea voyages. When he was fourteen he attended boarding school, then went on to Harvard Law School. After graduating he worked for a New York City law firm before entering politics with the dream of following in Theodore Roosevelt's footsteps.

Overcoming Great Odds

Hopes of running for New York governor dimmed when he contracted poliomyelitis—polio—and lost the use of his legs at the age of thirty-nine. At the time, no one knew what caused polio, commonly called infantile paralysis because it usually infected children. It was the most dreaded disease in America because it paralyzed the arms, legs, or entire body. No one knew how to treat it and many polio victims died. After rehabilitation, Roosevelt regained strength in his hands, arms, and back. Though his legs improved a little, he could never again walk without braces and crutches.

In spite of this, he aggressively campaigned and won election as governor in 1929, the same year Herbert Hoover became president. On January 1, 1929, Roosevelt was sworn in as governor of New York in the very room where he had watched his cousin take the oath of office. Roosevelt had thwarted the rumors that he was unfit for the job of governor because he was handicapped. He had traveled throughout New York, visiting every county and averaging six speeches a day.

Franklin Roosevelt was a charismatic, or charming, leader. His leadership stemmed from surrounding himself with the best advisors he could find, according to James A. Farley. Farley served as Roosevelt's campaign manager in his 1930 campaign for reelection as governor of New York and also managed Roosevelt's 1932 presidential campaign.[4] While governor, Roosevelt established an unemployment relief system. Since it was the first of its kind, it gained Roosevelt national acclaim. During his campaign for president, this program was used to show Roosevelt as a caring reformer.

Identifying With the Common Man

Roosevelt's 1932 election speeches pointed out programs President Hoover had suggested in 1923 while serving as secretary of commerce, yet did not exercise during his term as president. Among these suggestions were the reduction of work hours per week and the provision of temporary work by the federal government in time of crisis.[5] Roosevelt's statewide relief program for New York included some of these suggestions.

This caring attitude translated to concern for the common man, which helped him win the presidential election in 1932. Perhaps he identified with the common man because he had worked so hard to master his handicap before campaigning for governor of New York in 1929. He seemed to understand the pain, struggle, and humiliation of the common man during the Great Depression. His fight to overcome his handicap resulted in learning to walk with braces and crutches. He hid this fact whenever possible so Americans would not think him weak. Roosevelt's lack of mobility due to his legs did not hinder his motivation. Nor did it hinder the belief of those around him that Roosevelt was the right man for the job.

Farley said over radio station WEAF the night of the 1932 presidential election,

> I think that the people are happy today at the prospect of an administration by a fresh mind, by a man whose long experience as the governor of the Empire State has taught him what government is all about, and one whose public service has given him faith in his intelligence, his capacity and his high sense of duty.[6]

Presidential Inauguration

Though he was following his cousin to the White House, Roosevelt was not riding the coattails of a family name. He brought with him from his post as

SOURCE DOCUMENT

THE MONEY CHANGERS HAVE FLED FROM THEIR HIGH SEATS IN THE TEMPLE OF OUR CIVILIZATION. WE MAY NOW RESTORE THAT TEMPLE TO THE ANCIENT TRUTHS. THE MEASURE OF THE RESTORATION LIES IN THE EXTENT TO WHICH WE APPLY SOCIAL VALUES MORE NOBLE THAN MERE MONETARY PROFIT. HAPPINESS LIES NOT IN THE MERE POSSESSION OF MONEY; IT LIES IN THE JOY OF ACHIEVEMENT, IN THE THRILL OF CREATIVE EFFORT.[7]

This quote is from Franklin D. Roosevelt's inaugural address given on March 4, 1933.

governor of New York at least two programs that would help pull the nation out of the Great Depression—work relief and the Civilian Conservation Corps (CCC). Both programs bolstered self-worth by providing jobs with regular wages, as opposed to placing the jobless on "the dole," or welfare (the handout of funds from the government). The CCC was designed for young, unmarried men to work in the state parks, helping plant trees and fight forest fires.

He also brought with him a group of university professors and advisors who shared his beliefs. Because most of the group were scholars, and Roosevelt trusted them for solid advice, they became known as the "Brain Trust" while Roosevelt was governor of New York. This group of men advised him while he campaigned for governor and for president. The New Deal reflected their beliefs that the

Depression was not due to personal or moral failure, but the result of economic disorder. The Brain Trust's ideas and suggested programs focused on a theory of cooperation. The federal government, industry and state leaders, and individual Americans needed to cooperate in order to pull the United States out of economic disorder.[8]

Roosevelt became known as a friend of the common people, the so-called forgotten man, and he kept America informed on the nation's progress through radio addresses. As fiercely as he worked to pull America from the grip of the Depression, Roosevelt also worked at hiding the reality of his handicap. To the American people he was someone who had courageously battled polio and overcame it. In reality, Roosevelt orchestrated elaborate deceptions to make it appear in public as if he could walk. In truth, he remained completely paralyzed from the waist down.

Those who knew Roosevelt were divided into two camps: Those who liked Roosevelt described him as smart, at times even wily; those who did not like him described him as deceptive or manipulative. Whether his contemporaries liked him or not, they saw Roosevelt was an optimistic man. When compared with the low spirits of President Hoover's final day, Roosevelt was an appealing alternative.

Roosevelt knew what was at stake as he took over the presidency. Friends and associates voiced their opinion that Roosevelt was destined to become the greatest president the United States ever had—if his plans succeeded. A close friend told him that if he failed, he would be known as the worst president ever. "If I fail," Roosevelt replied, "I shall be the last one [president]."[9]

A Spirit of Cooperation

United Press White House reporter Thomas Stokes quoted a leading Republican congressman's opinion of the new president: "My, that man is refreshing after Hoover! . . . He was courteous. He deferred here and there. He was good-humored. But all the way through he kept a straight line toward what he wanted. When it was all over, he had got his way. He's smart!"[10]

In truth, Roosevelt was a curious blend of smart, shrewd, and controlling. He was a professional who understood how to make people work together and he did what it took to gain their cooperation. Cooperation among branches of government, both state and federal, was the basis of the New Deal. Cooperation was needed to change the country's circumstances. And circumstances in 1932 demanded drastic changes in the role of the federal government. As president, Roosevelt was in place to oversee this transformation—one of the most dramatic in American history.[11]

6

THE FIRST ONE HUNDRED DAYS

What we need in Washington is less fact finding and more thinking.[1]

—Franklin D. Roosevelt, campaign speech in Boston, October 31, 1932

Roosevelt got right to work on the promises he had made during his campaign—to bring relief to the unemployed, help the farmers, and balance the budget. He did not arrive at the White House with a single, clear plan for fulfilling his New Deal. Instead, he focused on "the three Rs"— relief, recovery, and reform.

The first one hundred days of Roosevelt's administration were a whirlwind of activity. He immediately called for a bank holiday to protect funds from panicked withdrawals. While the banks were closed, auditors reviewed the books. They reopened only those banks they felt were financially stable.

Roosevelt also called a special session of Congress to address ways to turn the economy around. One of the first acts passed by Congress was the Emergency Banking Act. It removed the United States from the

The boy pictured is a miner's child from Scott's Run, West Virginia. Using his pick he would dig through the snow for coal. Whatever coal he found would be burned to keep the house warm. Though the ground is snow-covered, he is not wearing shoes.

gold standard. The American dollar was no longer redeemable in gold. This act allowed the federal government to have greater control of the supply and value of the dollar.[2] Congress felt that past banking practices in large part caused the Great Depression. A series of acts created government control of banking at the federal level.

The Glass-Steagall Banking Act of 1933 specified that banks could only collect funds to be held in accounts for depositors or serve as investment banks. Investment banks bought and sold securities (stocks and bonds) in the stock market. Prior to the stock market crash, banks did both, often losing the money of depositors.

Chatting with the Nation

One week after his inauguration, President Roosevelt explained on the radio to the American public all that was happening. He explained the banking crisis and his solution in terms the average person could understand. He explained how the banking industry worked, and its importance in keeping the wheels of other industries turning. He also explained how the rush on banks by depositors to withdraw money caused banks to fold. Most Americans used banks as a place to deposit funds and write checks on their accounts. Few realized that deposited funds were invested in mortgages and loans to other bankers.

Roosevelt assured listeners that each reopened bank was now a secure place for people to place their money. He encouraged people to resume banking. Listeners felt the president spoke directly to them, in a conversational and friendly tone. This first radio broadcast on March 12, 1933, was followed by thirty sporadic radio updates, which came to be known as fireside chats.[3]

By June 22, the banking crisis was over and individual deposits were insured. The Federal Deposit Insurance Corporation (FDIC), which is still in place today, insured individual accounts up to $100,000. If an insured bank failed, FDIC paid off the account if another bank did not buy out the failed bank. People could trust banks again. To encourage people to invest in the stock market once again, the Truth-in-Securities Act was passed in 1933. This law gave investors the right to full and accurate financial information about the stock purchased and the firm issuing the stock. Congress added a regulation to curb unfair stock market practices and govern the sale of stocks through the Federal Securities Act of 1933.[4] It placed federal control over stocks and bonds sold in more than one state. The Federal Trade Commission (FTC) was set up to regulate the act. Later, further federal control created the Securities Exchange Act. It protected people from buying unsafe stocks and bonds. It replaced the Federal Securities Act in 1934. The FTC was replaced by the Securities and Exchange Commission (SEC) to oversee securities regulations.

During the first two weeks Roosevelt was in office, special acts and bills passed through the House and Senate on a daily basis. The president's advisors worked day and night to find possible solutions to the nation's economic crisis. The special session of Congress lasted exactly one hundred days. At its adjournment, a broad spectrum of laws and programs were in place to combat the Depression. In this flurry of activity that launched his New Deal domestic reform program, Roosevelt boosted morale by asking Congress to ratify the Twenty-first Amendment to revoke Prohibition. (The sale of beer, wine and other liquor had become illegal after the Eighteenth Amendment to the Constitution was enacted in 1920.) Congress also passed fifteen major bills, including the Emergency Banking Act, and established the Agricultural Adjustment Administration and the National Recovery Administration.[5]

Agricultural Adjustment Administration

To address the national economic crisis, the Agricultural Adjustment Administration (AAA) was created in May 1933 to assist farmers. The goal of the AAA was to raise farm product prices by limiting production. The AAA raised funds by taxing processors of farm products. Wheat, used to make flour, and milk were paid for by the flour mills and milk bottlers. Their final product was also taxed. Anything produced from farm products—canned goods, frozen vegetables, cereal, dairy products—was taxed. The AAA used the funds raised through these taxes to support farmers. Farmers were paid to limit production by not planting

In the 1930s, a young Oklahoma girl works as a migrant worker in Salina Valley in Monterey County, California. After picking peas all day, her hamper full of peas is checked before she receives a ticket for payment.

crops on part of their land.[6]

This plan increased farm income. Rather than having excess crops they could not sell, farmers were able to sell what they grew. They also earned a little extra for helping to balance supply and demand. Supply (goods available for sale) and demand (the quantity customers want and are willing to buy) needs to equal out. When there is too little supply, prices go up. When there is too much, prices go down. By limiting production, the AAA hoped to help balance demand—and price—to meet supply. Eventually, fewer goods would bring prices up while also increasing demand, the AAA reasoned.

Through funding from AAA, farmers no longer demonstrated their plight by spilling gallons of milk across the roadways or by burning corn for fuel because it was more abundant than coal. As far as the farmers were concerned, the government had at least noticed their problems. Those who still had their farms when the AAA was created were still struggling. Most had struggled since the end of World War I, when demand for their crops lessened. Farm debts mounted when crop yields did not earn more than the cash spent to plant crops. Unable to sell all their crops, farmers were left no choice but to accept lower prices for what they did grow.

It did not take long for people to wonder how this plan to help farmers fit into the nation's recovery from the Great Depression. After all, there were hundreds of people in cities and in migrant work camps who needed food and clothing. People wondered why the government would pay farmers to limit production. It was the old theory of supply and demand meant to regulate prices. The lower the supply of crops, the higher the demand. Since demand became high, crop prices rose, helping farmers make money to provide for their families.

National Recovery Administration

To address the needs of the unemployed, the president and his advisors focused on helping industry and labor create fair business practices. Established in June 1933, the National Industrial Recovery Act was one of the most important of the new laws. This act created the National Recovery Administration (NRA) to enforce codes of fair practices for business and industry. Representatives of firms within each industry helped write the codes.[7]

AN ACT TO ENCOURAGE NATIONAL INDUSTRIAL RECOVERY, TO FOSTER FAIR COMPETITION, AND TO PROVIDE FOR THE CONSTRUCTION OF CERTAIN USEFUL PUBLIC WORKS, AND FOR OTHER PURPOSES.

TITLE

I–INDUSTRIAL RECOVERY

DECLARATION OF POLICY

SEC. 1. A NATIONAL EMERGENCY PRODUCTIVE OF WIDESPREAD UNEMPLOYMENT AND DISORGANIZATION OF INDUSTRY, WHICH BURDENS INTERSTATE AND FOREIGN COMMERCE, AFFECTS THE PUBLIC WELFARE, AND UNDERMINES THE STANDARDS OF LIVING OF THE AMERICAN PEOPLE, IS HEREBY DECLARED TO EXIST. IT IS HEREBY DECLARED TO BE THE POLICY OF CONGRESS TO REMOVE OBSTRUCTIONS TO THE FREE FLOW OF INTERSTATE AND FOREIGN COMMERCE WHICH TEND TO DIMINISH THE AMOUNT THEREOF; AND TO PROVIDE FOR THE GENERAL WELFARE BY PROMOTING THE ORGANIZATION OF INDUSTRY FOR THE PURPOSE OF COOPERATIVE ACTION AMONG TRADE GROUPS, TO INDUCE AND MAINTAIN UNITED ACTION OF LABOR AND MANAGEMENT UNDER ADEQUATE GOVERNMENTAL SANCTIONS AND SUPERVISION, TO ELIMINATE UNFAIR COMPETITIVE PRACTICES, TO PROMOTE THE FULLEST POSSIBLE UTILIZATION OF THE PRESENT PRODUCTIVE CAPACITY OF INDUSTRIES, TO AVOID UNDUE RESTRICTION OF PRODUCTION (EXCEPT AS MAY BE TEMPORARILY REQUIRED), TO INCREASE THE CONSUMPTION OF INDUSTRIAL AND AGRICULTURAL PRODUCTS BY INCREASING PURCHASING POWER, TO REDUCE AND RELIEVE UNEMPLOYMENT, TO IMPROVE STANDARDS OF LABOR, AND OTHERWISE TO REHABILITATE INDUSTRY AND TO CONSERVE NATURAL RESOURCES.[8]

The National Industrial Recovery Act was passed on June 16, 1933.

The codes were designed to aid business by allowing member firms to set standards of quality and production. In the windows of stores and businesses throughout the country, the emblem of the eagle with the NRA logo was displayed. This meant that company followed the codes established by the NRA, such as offering minimum wages and fair maximum hours for a workweek. It meant the company supported the right of workers to join unions. It also meant the company worked to set the lowest price possible for goods. People not only would want to work for NRA companies, but also buy products from them.

Low prices for goods meant purchasing power increased. People's wages now went a little farther. Wages were also more consistent. In the past, a business owner could charge large sums for his products but pay his employee very little. If the employee wanted the job, he would take the wages offered. If the business could not sell what they made—because people could not afford it—workers might get laid off. Prior to the New Deal programs, workers who were "let go" because of production lows received no compensation or benefits as they do today. They were simply left unemployed. During the Great Depression, many people were walking the streets looking for work, selling apples or pencils on street corners, or waiting in the long lines at soup kitchens.

Necessary Action

At the close of Roosevelt's first one hundred days in office, most of the nation was feeling a little relief. However, people still felt confident that recovery was in sight. They saw that recovery would come about through reform. The NRA highlighted all three of these ideas. If the economy was not yet improved, people's spirits were by the activity taking place at the nation's capital. Not even during the critical administrations of George Washington and Abraham Lincoln had so many significant and far-reaching plans been enacted so quickly. Roosevelt entered the White House with the idea that action—any action—was necessary and he worked to set laws in motion. Of the fifteen major bills he pushed through Congress, only two were his own ideas—the Economy Act and the Civilian Conservation Corps. Yet the fact that all fifteen bills became law was a feat in itself. Never before had any president worked so rapidly and with such fierce determination for action.[9] In light of later developments, Roosevelt may have been the only president to deliver more programs than he actually promised. These programs put men to work, provided relief for the unemployed, and helped the farmers.[10]

Franklin D. Roosevelt "became the standard by which we measure our chief executives and by which they, Democrat and Republican, measure themselves," stated Dr. Patrick J. Maney, professor of history at Tulane University in New Orleans. "We even use Roosevelt's first one hundred days in office as a benchmark to assess the early performance of our new Presidents. And if they don't perform Rooseveltian feats during their first hundred days, we declare them failures."[11]

Most Americans appreciated Roosevelt's decisive actions. In the presence of a man who could not walk, America was finding the power to get back on its feet.[12] His critics, however, called his programs "creeping socialism." Some even feared the New Deal programs would lead to communism. Many people confused the two terms. Socialism is founded on collective ownership. The public owns all land, factories, and resources as a means for equal treatment for all members of society. Communism focuses on government ownership and regulation of all resources. Both were opposed to the so-called "selfishness" the free-enterprise, or capitalist, system encouraged. The New Deal was trying to maintain the free-enterprise system while finding ways to ride out the economic slump of the Great Depression. Secretary of the Interior Harold Ickes summed up the prevailing mood of the American people: "It's more than a New Deal," he said. "It's a new world."[13]

ABCs OF REFORM

Roosevelt's administration had won the first round in its match against the Great Depression. By focusing on the three R's—relief, recovery, and reform—the president's administration was well on its way to improving morale and promoting economic growth. The Federal Emergency Relief Act (FERA) provided grants to each of the forty-eight states making up the nation in 1939 (Alaska and Hawaii were not yet states). These grants provided relief funds for the unemployed. Most people had not been exposed to the dole, or charity, before, and many had a difficult time accepting government handouts. Harry Hopkins, emergency relief administrator, suggested to President Roosevelt that work in exchange for pay would be easier for people to swallow.[2]

Harold Ickes, secretary of the interior, wrote in his diary on November 6, 1933:

At twelve o'clock Secretaries [Henry] Wallace [Secretary of Agriculture] and [Frances] Perkins [Secretary of Labor], and Harry Hopkins, Emergency Relief Administrator, came in for a conversation by direction of the President. Professor Rogers [one of the Brain Trust] was also here at the suggestion of Secretary Wallace. We discussed a plan of Hopkins to put anywhere from two to four million men back to work for standard wages on a thirty-hour-week basis. He would continue to pay on account of these wages what he is now contributing toward relief, and the balance would be made up out of the public works funds.[3]

Title II of the National Industrial Recovery Act (NIRA) called for creation of the Public Works Administration (PWA). The PWA was placed under the direction of Ickes. He and Hopkins used the plan to put America's unemployed people back to work. Many of the programs created by Roosevelt's administration clung to this philosophy of work in exchange for relief, becoming federally funded work programs. The driving force behind them was that the American people needed to feel wanted and be productive. And they were right. "It makes us feel like an American citizen to earn our own living. Being on the dole or relief roll makes us lazy and the funds are not enough to live decent on. We are thankful for what we receive though," Works Progress Administration (WPA) workers in Battle Creek, Michigan, wrote to President Roosevelt.[4]

Life was slowly improving as employment figures climbed slightly. But some of the New Deal plans did not fully succeed. Farmers still struggled to keep their farms, even with the AAA. Supply and demand had not yet balanced out. The rather disjointed Civil Works Administration was replaced by the more focused WPA in 1934. The supply of apples and pencils for the unemployed to sell on street corners was met with confusion. Many people thought they were only for the unemployed to buy.[5] But, despite problems, Roosevelt explained that his theory was to at least try something: "The country needs and, unless I mistake its temper, the country demands bold, persistent experimentation. It is common sense to take a method and try it; if it fails, admit it frankly and try another. But above all, try something."[6]

Brainstorming

Many people think Roosevelt himself came up with the many programs that encompassed the New Deal. Actually, he came up with the routine used to devise these plans. He asked his private council to brainstorm ideas until they had programs reasonable enough to put into action. The group was ever-changing, but at times included: his longtime aide, Louis McHenry Howe; James Farley, postmaster general; Edward M. House, American statesman and former advisor to Woodrow Wilson; and Columbia University professors, Raymond Moley, Rexford Guy Tugwell, and Adolf A. Berle, Jr. Among the most influential of the group were Moley, Tugwell, and Berle. The president proposed ideas which the Brain Trust then discussed, debated, and changed until the plans met the president's philosophy. They considered how big business would view a plan, how the plan would be implemented, and whether a plan would work for the average laborer. With enough trial and error, his advisors concluded, a crevice in the shell of the economic depression would eventually be found. Once located, and pried wider, the shell was bound to crack and the nation would experience renewed hope and growth.

People came to picture the New Deal programs as the result of a sort of academic brainstorm. Political cartoons depicted a sickly looking group of old professors huddled around a table. Whether meant as a humorous or hostile portrayal depended on which side a person camped—in favor of the New Deal or against it. In most cases, the image was meant to poke fun because people wondered how such programs would help. Many worried that America was headed for the socialism spreading across Europe. After all, from this side of the ocean, socialism seemed to consist of the government stepping in to control aspects of business and daily living. To some this was exactly what the president was trying to do with his work programs.

"If, let us say, the government of the United States, forgetting about the Constitution, were to commandeer everything and every one tomorrow afternoon," wrote Adolf A. Berle, Jr., a leading member of the Brain Trust, about six months after Roosevelt took office, then Americans could worry the country was headed in the same direction as much of Europe. And he admitted it was within the power of those in office. "If there is a general breakdown, [the American government] will have to do, temporarily at least, something very like this; but it is the last resort; a counsel of despair; an indication that we cannot run our private lives effectively enough to solve the situation."[7]

The president's refusal to nationalize the banking system demonstrated the policy of the New Deal. The intent was to salvage the country's economy, not revolutionize it. Through experimentation and cooperation between the federal and state governments, the Roosevelt administration sought to balance the federal budget and provide temporary public works and relief programs.[8]

"The policies which are spoken of as new have an entirely honorable lineage in American History; they are an expression of the American faith," wrote Rexford G. Tugwell, a Brain Trust member, in the April 1935, *Atlantic Monthly*.[9] In addition, many programs stemmed from those Herbert Hoover had recommended while secretary of commerce in 1923.

Roosevelt's Tree Army

One of the first programs started was the Civilian Conservation Corps (CCC). This was one of Roosevelt's own ideas. He had successfully implemented a similar plan while he was governor of New York. The CCC put young men from needy families to work at useful conservation projects, such as planting trees and building dams. "I owe the CCC a lot," one recruit told his instructor. "I went in as a boy and came out a man."[10] Young men eighteen years old and up went to work in reforestation programs. They lived in tent camps. The CCC kept them busy planting trees, clearing land for road building, and working to improve national and state parks.

The first camp opened in George Washington National Forest in Virginia on April 17, 1933. The goal of the program was to have a quarter of a million enrollees. This goal was met by July 1, 1933, with combined enrollments at over thirteen hundred camps spread across the nation.

"The boys are settled in groups of 200 in 1,330 different camps, and the work is well underway," wrote Dorothy D. Bromley in a July 23, 1933, *New York Times* article. "The 25,000 war veterans who were enrolled on June 26 will soon be established in camps of their own, bringing the grand total of C.C.C. camps to 1,438."[11]

Though run by the army, by either a regular officer or by a reserve officer called to active duty, the camps were civilian in character. The young men learned first aid, personal cleanliness, and the rudiments of sanitation. They had morning calisthenics and served rotating kitchen duty, called KP [kitchen patrol].

"There is no military discipline in the C.C.C., no saluting, no standing at attention. There is not supposed to be any drilling, either, although the boys in this camp [in George Washington National Forest, Virginia] asked for a little, so that they could make a showing in the Fourth of July parades," Bromley reported.[12]

Civilian Conservation Corps enrollees sometimes traded pickax for shovel when forest fires blazed. These CCC *workers are on the fire line of a big forest fire in the West.*

Not only did these young men plant trees, dig ditches, and clear land for roadways, they fought forest fires and built the cabins and recreational facilities that are still in use at many national forests, parks, and state and national campgrounds. By the end of 1933, an educational advisor was stationed at each camp. The men were encouraged to take classes at night to earn high school diplomas and learn skills such as welding. Camps were eventually added for older men, veterans, and American Indians. The CCC, one of the longest running of the New Deal programs, was credited with improving the morale, health, and education of millions of young men, as well as instilling in these young men a sense of pride in America.[13]

Alphabet Soup

The CCC may be one of the New Deal's most popular and memorable programs, but it was far from being the only large-scale program. The Public Works Administration (PWA) created jobs for large numbers of people. Thousands of schools, courthouses, bridges, dams, and other useful projects were built through the PWA. The Home Owners Loan Corporation (HOLC) provided money at low interest for people struggling to pay mortgages. The Tennessee Valley Authority (TVA) built many dams to control floods and to provide electricity for residents of the Tennessee River Valley. Many of the programs implemented during Roosevelt's administration were referred to by their acronyms—TVA, CCC, PWA. The press came to call these programs "alphabet soup," and jokingly referred to the president as FDR. The nickname stuck.

FDR's programs were designed not only to reform the economy, but to deal with issues affecting families and the morale of Americans. For instance, as the Depression wore on, fewer children were attending school. Some were unable to go because they had no clothes to wear. Others left school to try to find work, or felt the future was hopeless and dropped out. For many who had made it through high school, college was an unaffordable dream.

Harold Ickes wrote in his diary on January 24, 1934,

The Secretary of Labor, Harry L. Hopkins, Dr. [George] Zook, Commissioner of Education, and I

Public Works Administration workers building this dam in Bonneville, Oregon, were under pressure. They rushed to finish the spillway piers to keep ahead of an expected crest of flood waters as the river rose.

had a conference with the President at noon about the educational situation. On account of the depression many thousands of children are being denied educational opportunities in the schools. Many schools are running on part time and thousands of teachers are either unemployed or, if employed, work at salaries, which, if paid, are mere pittances.[14]

The president directed Hopkins to remedy the problem. Students must have help to stay in school and go on to college. As part of the PWA, consolidated schools should be built where facilities were poor or nonexistent.

The Depression was not all gloom. The National Youth Administration provided recreational opportunities for young people. Here, a couple dances the jitterbug to a popular tune in Oakland, California.

One result of Hopkins's efforts was the National Youth Administration (NYA). Students in high school and college were provided with work-study projects. For instance, in addition to traditional classes, young women learned typing and office skills while young men learned mechanics. "Sometimes I typed almost all night and had to deliver it to school the next morning," Helen Farmer recalled. "This was a good program. It got necessary work done. It gave teenagers a chance to work for pay. Mine bought me clothes and shoes, school supplies, some movies and mad money."[15]

As NYA policies evolved, students received career guidance, job training, and cultural and educational enrichment programs. The NYA also provided recreational opportunities. Many students attended NYA-run camps during school vacations.[16]

Carrie Johnson of Winnsboro, South Carolina, said,

> I got a notice to go to the NYA. Mrs. Ford was foreman. A crowd of girls, most of them younger than me, sewed every day. . . . We could sew on whatever materials Mrs. Ford could get for us. Mrs. Wright, they called her attendance officer for the schools, brought bolts and bolts of the prettiest soft cotton cloth. It was pink, blue, peach, and lavender. I enjoyed making up all kinds of little dresses, sacks, wrappers, and everything.[17]

OPPOSING THE NEW DEAL

I ask you to purge the man who claims to be a Democrat, from the Democratic Party, and I mean Franklin Double-Crossing Roosevelt.[1]

—Father Charles Coughlin,
the "radio priest," 1936

By 1934, the spirit of the people and the economy had improved a little. Many people still struggled, though, and letters poured into the White House, addressed to the president, the first lady, and leaders of various agencies, asking for help. "We are completely out of coal and how can he [her husband] work without no food or clothes. I don't see how times are going to get better if men have to work for so low wages and food stuffs so high, and rent has raised,"[2] one woman wrote to Harry Hopkins, who was in charge of the WPA.

An Oklahoma woman sought help from the first lady, Eleanor Roosevelt: "We are all barefooted. And no clothes to wear. and Can not Send our children to School. Thy [sic] put us off the relief in July and. my Husband. Cant get back on. . . . it is hard to try and feed 8 children on bread & milk and. part of the time no bread. . . . the poor class of people down here is treated like dogs."[3]

Many letters complained about how the programs were run. Others accused the president of doing nothing to stop unfair practices. An anonymous person from Brooklyn, New York, wrote,

> When you took office it was your goodness of heart to help those who could not help themselves, but since 1933 we who need help are the ones who are not getting it, and those who do not are . . . That is why I have written to you to clean up the bad spots otherwise, I am afraid reelection will not be forthcoming because they will blame you and Not Harry Hopkins.[4]

It was not only the common man who felt frustrated with the work relief and other programs. Businessmen wanted to run their businesses as they had before the stock market crash. The NRA program, though, created long lists of rules they had to follow. "Mr. Roosevelt proposed in his speech that the NRA and a lot of these other government regulated business ethics would be made permanent," humorist Will Rogers stated in his January 4, 1934, column. "Well that was a terrible blow to some business men. They had figured they would only be required to be honest by the government till the emergency was over."[5]

Poking Fun at FDR

Roosevelt was so popular throughout the nation that he was named *Time* magazine Man of the Year for 1934. But, five years into the Great Depression,

America had not regained the prosperity of the 1920s. James Farley, one of President Roosevelt's political advisors, sent a clipping to the president about a worker who had fallen while resting on his shovel handle and broken his wrist. Farley suggested that the president supply "non-skid handles" for future projects.[6] But Mr. Donner (full name unavailable) had a different opinion about so-called shovel-leaners:

> Many of the men working as common laborers haven't been accustomed to hard physical labor; a good proportion of them have large families to support on their earnings of $12 a week and are always undernourished. And the men shouldn't be expected to do $25 worth of work for $12.[7]

Donner understood. He was a former business owner who started on work relief early in the Depression. He was eventually promoted to timekeeper, tracking each man's hours at local WPA projects.

Other WPA workers did not have any skills at all. Working as laborers was all they could do. They worried over rumors that the WPA and other agencies would close down for lack of funding. Others felt frustration that they did not earn enough through relief work. "We do not believe that you are to blame for the way the relief work is being run," a letter-writer from Jasper, Alabama, told the president,

> We know you have lots of sympathy for the poor downtrodden undernourished poor of this whole U.S.A. There are numbers of people though who do

This political cartoon mocks union workers along with the New Deal. While Uncle Sam tries to open a door, an unaware husky worker, tagged "Ill-Advised Labor," leans against the other side of the door.

think that you know how we are treated and seem to think that you are just letting the wealthy who have control of the relief work do as they please with caring for the poor.[8]

The poor still could not seem to make ends meet. Those who were getting by were also getting the work relief they did not seem to need. And those who had money worried that these work relief programs were not at all temporary. Despite the controversy over the many programs launched by President Roosevelt, most workers were grateful to have work. When a group of WPA workers in Maryland wrote to the president for help in getting timely payments and better wages, they thanked him for all he had done for them. "The majority of us men gave you our votes and we are intending to again at this election. And we are thanking you for the good you have done us,"[9] one WPA worker wrote in his letter to President Roosevelt.

Father Coughlin

People continued to write to the president informing him of their hardship and the corruption within the New Deal agencies. But Father Charles Coughlin, a Catholic priest at the Shrine of the Little Flower in a suburb of Detroit, Michigan, received even more mail than the president.[10] Through his "Golden Hour of the Little Flower" radio broadcasts, Coughlin had a following of around 30 million listeners. While he had once told people "It is either Roosevelt or ruin,"[11] Coughlin now spoke poorly of President Roosevelt over the airwaves. Despite the programs enacted by the New Deal, Coughlin blamed the president for the continued Depression.

By November 1934, Coughlin established the National Union for Social Justice. "I knew that if anyone was going to inform the American citizenry of the truth it would have to be me. After all, I knew from the letters I was receiving that the people trusted me and would believe me when I spoke."[12] Though Coughlin favored the rights of workers to organize, calling this industrial democracy, he disliked FDR's policies to control the value of the dollar. He was also strongly against U.S. membership in a world court—a proposal to create an international high court. In a 1936 radio broadcast, Coughlin lashed out against FDR at his strongest: "The great betrayer and liar, Franklin D. Roosevelt, who promised to drive the money changers from the temple, has succeeded in driving the farmers from their homesteads and the citizens from their homes in the cities."[13] Coughlin portrayed FDR as only pretending to side with the common man.

Big Business

Though Coughlin worked to undermine the efforts of the New Deal, he was a staunch advocate of unions. Where companies opposed unions, strikes were the answer. These strikes often resulted in violence and bloodshed. Employees had the right under NRA to unionize, but employers tried to scare them from organizing. Labor organizers planned more strikes designed to shut down companies until union shops were established. Employers banded together in opposition to the strikers. During 1934, 1,800 strikes involving nearly 1.5 million workers took place.[14] In July 1934, the Teamsters—a union of truckers, chauffeurs, and warehouse workers—tried to organize the longshoremen (workers who loaded and unloaded cargo onto ships) in San Francisco. Violence between the workers and police called in by the companies resulted in gunfire which left two strikers dead and many others wounded.[15]

Not everyone suffered during the Depression. A small percentage of families lost most of their fortunes but they did not become destitute during the early years of the Depression. These people, together with industry owners, found great fault with FDR's federal assistance. They argued that relief programs encouraged people to be lazy. Those in big business and industry saw the New Deal agencies as creating dependence rather than helping people improve their lives. By 1935, most of the New Deal programs came under attack. Opponents charged that these agencies were raising the expectations of the poor. Billions of dollars were spent creating jobs to improve the economy, yet out of a labor force of 52 million Americans, 11 million were still unemployed in 1935.[16] Anger and resentment resulted.

Besides balking at unions, big business disliked efforts to establish a minimum wage and set a maximum workweek. Until the Great Depression settled upon America, the average workweek consisted of six days. The average number of hours varied depending upon the industry and the amount of work that needed to be done. In an effort to create fair, competitive business practices, the NRA created standards of operation. It also pushed for a thirty-hour workweek in an effort to spread the amount of available work among more people. Before the Depression, the standard workweek was six days and people often worked sixty hours or more. If people worked fewer hours, the president's advisors reasoned, more people could be employed to cover the workload.

Huey Long

While the president's administration worked to share the wealth of jobs, Huey Long, a U.S. senator from Louisiana, had a plan to "share the wealth" of society. Early in Roosevelt's administration, Long had tried to hamper the passing of the National Industrial Recovery Act but his fellow senators shouted him off the floor. Long now accused Roosevelt of favoring the banking interests and proposed his own plan to save the nation. The plan, called Share-Our-Wealth, involved pooling all personal fortunes over about $3 million and redistributing them among each family. His plan assured a two-thousand-dollar annual income for each family with five thousand dollars offered to aid in buying a home, a radio, and a car.[17] His plan also involved other attractive features such as establishing a minimum wage, old-age pensions, free college education to deserving students, and public works.

An effective slogan promoted his plan: "Every Man a King." Share-Our-Wealth clubs sprang up around the nation. By the beginning of 1935, Share-Our-Wealth claimed more than 27,431 clubs in every state throughout the nation and 4.6 million members.[18]

The plan also called for a system of taxes to prevent anyone in the country from earning more than $1 million in a year or accruing a fortune above $5 million.[19] The plan was far more radical than anything the Roosevelt administration had proposed, and many claimed it was thinly veiled socialism. Long claimed he was not against the free-enterprise system, but wanted to save it. "The Senator had no training in economics, and his knowledge of economic relationships was skimpy at best. In the end, economists dismissed Share-Our-Wealth as a hoax," according to historian David Bennett.[20]

Overruled

Throughout 1935, the United States Supreme Court heard a variety of cases involving industry versus individuals or businesses against the United States. In case after case, it seemed, the Supreme Court ruled against those people the National Recovery Administration was supposed to help. As the year wore on, the Supreme Court declared the National Industrial Recovery Act unconstitutional. The justices felt Congress had given too much power to the president in regulating the programs of business on a federal level. The role of the three branches of government— executive (the president), judicial (the Supreme Court and other federal courts), and legislative (the

Congress)—was intended to provide balance. NIRA, with its many rules, was equal to government-centralized business. The Supreme Court would no longer tolerate such a program.

"This is the end of this business of centralization," Justice Louis Brandeis told two of Roosevelt's aides, "and I want you to go back and tell the president that we're not going to let this government centralize everything. It's come to an end."[21]

This decision threatened to unravel the entire New Deal. The trouble was not limited to the NIRA, either. In January 1936, the Supreme Court declared that the processing tax imposed by the AAA was also unconstitutional. Funds totaling $200 million collected through this tax—and slated to support farmers and control crop production—was to be returned to the processors.[22] The Roosevelt administration's efforts to fund the program, not to mention balance the federal budget, collapsed along with the crop prices.

The Supreme Court did not stop there. As the year progressed, more acts and laws created by the New Deal were found to be unconstitutional. The New Deal was two years old and yet the Depression wore on. With every decision of the Supreme Court, the Roosevelt administration scrambled to rescue threatened programs. With a new election year approaching, FDR took action.

9

THE SECOND ONE HUNDRED DAYS

The dogmas of the quiet past are inadequate to the stormy present. . . . we must think anew, and act anew. We must disenthrall ourselves, and then we shall save our country.[1]

—Abraham Lincoln

The decisions of the Supreme Court weighed heavily on morale because people were still feeling the Depression too deeply. Those with relief work worried it would be cut due to Supreme Court rulings. Others complained that the programs were run by corrupt bosses. Letters flooded the White House and government agencies asking for help. Some compared the Depression to slavery and looked to Roosevelt as a second Lincoln. One letter writer, from Liberty, Pennsylvania, told Eleanor Roosevelt:

> I am one of your greatest admirers but things are so bad everywhere. People don't have the wherewith to procure the necessities of Life. We are just slaves and how we hoped and trusted that Mr. Roosevelt would be another Lincoln and free us from the slavery that we are in today.[2]

To counter the damage done by the Supreme Court, and in preparation for reelection, Roosevelt launched a second period of frenzied activity similar to his first hundred days. Historians called this period the "Second One Hundred Days" or the "Second New Deal" because several instrumental relief laws were passed.

Revise and Strengthen

Each program that the Supreme Court overruled needed to be revised and reintroduced. Other programs were strengthened. FDR's administration and his Brain Trust now worked with renewed effort. All brainstorming also included plans to "court-proof" future agencies. What was working? The work projects of the PWA and WPA provided jobs constructing highways, bridges, streets, parks, and buildings. The bigger question was: What needed improvement?

NIRA had been beneficial and presidential advisors suggested revising it to strengthen the protections of collective bargaining. The National Labor Relations Act (NLRA), also called the Wagner Act, incorporated many of the provisions of the now invalidated NIRA. Workers had broad rights to organize into unions. Instead of allowing the agency heads (FDR's administrators) to enforce the rules, NLRA called for the creation of the National Labor Relations Board. The NLRB enforced and supported the rights it promised workers.[3] At first Roosevelt refused to support the Wagner Act. He wanted changes made. The final version of the act allowed workers to organize into unions and obligated employers to accept these unions. Representatives from the unions had the right to bargain with employers for the union members as a collective body. This was called collective bargaining. The bill, passed on July 5, 1935, was a significant victory for organized labor.[4]

The sweeping arm of the New Deal reached out not only to employ, but to educate and entertain. The Works Progress Administration (later renamed the Work Projects Administration in 1939), established to oversee a variety of building and renovation projects, also created jobs for writers, artists, musicians, and actors. About 8.5 million people were employed through WPA projects. The Federal Music Project presented low-cost or free concerts across the United States. The Federal Theatre Project employed 1,300 people, reaching over 25 million people through 1,200 productions.[5] The Federal Art Project produced hundreds of murals and thousands of paintings, many of which decorated buildings put up by the New Deal programs. The Federal Art Project also hired photographers to record the nation's history. Photography emerged as an important art form through this segment of the WPA while nurturing the creative talents of Dorothea Lange, Margaret Bourke-White, and Walker Evans, among others. The Federal Writers' Program hired writers to record the oral histories of people across the country, as well as create plays and dramas of the times. Saul Bellow, Ralph Ellison, John Cheever, and Margaret Walker were a few of the now well-known writers employed by this program.[6]

Social Security

FDR's "Second Hundred Days" created agencies and programs that had a lasting impact on the nation. Among the most influential of these was Social Security. The Social Security Act provided pensions for the old, compensation for unemployed workers, and payments to the disabled and to needy children. People did not like the taxes taken from their payroll to cover Social Security. Roosevelt encouraged people to think of it as "being held in trust"[7] for their retirement, rather than thinking of it being used to fund retirement or unemployment benefits of other citizens.

The system was financed in two parts. For unemployment benefits, the employer paid a payroll tax

SOURCE DOCUMENT

AN ACT TO PROVIDE FOR THE GENERAL WELFARE BY ESTABLISHING A SYSTEM OF FEDERAL OLD-AGE BENEFITS, AND BY ENABLING THE SEVERAL STATES TO MAKE MORE ADEQUATE PROVISION FOR AGED PERSONS, BLIND PERSONS, DEPENDENT AND CRIPPLED CHILDREN, MATERNAL AND CHILD WELFARE, PUBLIC HEALTH, AND THE ADMINISTRATION OF THEIR UNEMPLOYMENT COMPENSATION LAWS; TO ESTABLISH A SOCIAL SECURITY BOARD; TO RAISE REVENUE; AND FOR OTHER PURPOSES.

BE IT ENACTED BY THE SENATE AND HOUSE OF REPRESENTATIVES OF THE UNITED STATES OF AMERICA IN CONGRESS ASSEMBLED.[8]

The Social Security Act was signed into law August 14, 1935.

SOURCE DOCUMENT

WE HAVE COME TO LEARN THAT THE LARGE MAJORITY OF OUR CITIZENS MUST HAVE PROTECTION AGAINST THE LOSS OF INCOME DUE TO UNEMPLOYMENT, OLD AGE, DEATH OF THE BREADWINNERS AND DISABLING ACCIDENT AND ILLNESS, NOT ONLY ON HUMANITARIAN GROUNDS, BUT IN THE INTEREST OF OUR NATIONAL WELFARE. IF WE ARE TO MAINTAIN A HEALTHY ECONOMY AND THRIVING PRODUCTION, WE NEED TO MAINTAIN THE STANDARD OF LIVING OF THE LOWER INCOME GROUPS IN OUR POPULATION WHO CONSTITUTE 90 PER CENT OF OUR PURCHASING POWER. . . .[9]

Frances Perkins, secretary of labor, comments on the Social Security Act during a national radio address on February 25, 1935.

for each employee. For Social Security benefits, equal contributions by employee and employer were made into the fund. Employee payments were deducted from the payroll check by the employer. Roosevelt admitted later that these payroll deductions were:

> . . . politics all the way through. We put those payroll contributions there so as to give the contributors a legal, moral, and political right to collect their pensions and their unemployment benefits. With those taxes in there, no damn politician can ever scrap my Social Security program.[10]

Soil Conservation

When the Supreme Court of the United States declared the AAA unconstitutional in 1936, the blow to the New Deal was twofold. In addition to returning funds collected from processors, the president's advisors needed a plan to continue aiding farmers. The Midwest was in bad shape. Dust storms raged across the southern Great Plains, damaging land from South Dakota to Texas. Worst hit were Kansas, Oklahoma, and parts of Texas, New Mexico, and Colorado. Decades of careless plowing and overgrazing along with a bad drought had stripped the Great Plains of their natural mantle of deep-rooted prairie grass. This set the scene for the worst agricultural disaster in American history, known as the Dust Bowl.

Advisors considered a plan to pay farmers to leave some land vacant as part of new soil conservation programs associated with the revised AAA. In addition, farmers worked with members of the Soil Erosion Service, part of the Interior Department, on methods of plowing to prevent soil erosion. This service also used the CCC for planting trees and working on other projects to stem the heavy erosion on the midwestern plains.[11]

In 1932, a prolonged drought had set in. The exposed soil grew steadily drier and more vulnerable to erosion, and in 1933, residents watched worriedly as fall winds churned up clouds of dust. According to Lawrence Svobida, a wheat farmer from Kansas,

A cloud is seen to be approaching from a distance of many miles. Already it has the banked appearance of a cumulus cloud, but it is black instead of white, and it

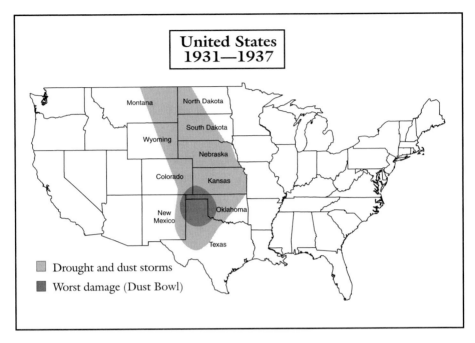

United States
1931—1937

Drought and dust storms
Worst damage (Dust Bowl)

This map shows the parts of the United States affected by drought and dust storms.

hangs low, seeming to hug the earth. Instead of being slow to change its form, it appears to be rolling on itself from the crest downward. As it sweeps onward, the landscape is progressively blotted out.[12]

The following spring was worse. Winds of up to sixty miles an hour howled across the prairie. The powdery soil rose two miles into the sky, burying livestock, blanketing houses, and filling mouths and lungs. In May, a two-day-long "black blizzard" scooped up 300 million tons of soil and carried it all the way to East Coast cities, including Washington, D.C., where the air was so thick with fine silt that the streetlights came on at midday.[13]

In 1934, the Shelterbelt Program was passed to set up wind blocks. Trees planted in small belts broke the force of damaging winds across the open plains. In 1935, the Soil Erosion Service was created to step up efforts to counter the devastation targeting the nation's farmers. Later, the Soil Erosion Service moved to the Department of Agriculture under the name Soil Conservation Service. In the meantime, it aided farmers in rescuing millions of acres of ruined countryside.[14]

10

DISCORD WITHIN

This generation of Americans has a rendezvous with destiny.[1]

—Franklin D. Roosevelt

Though the president and his advisors worked hard, the country seemed to remain in a sorry state. Battered from within by the slumped economy and opposition to the New Deal, the nation also faced setbacks from Mother Nature. Not only did dust storms afflict the Midwest between 1932 and 1938, but during 1936 alone, tornadoes, hurricanes, and floods caused property damage, took lives, and further crushed the morale of the nation. As FDR turned his attention to reelection, the Roosevelts experienced for themselves the setbacks from flood, winds, and erosion.

Campaign of 1936

During the election of 1936, Roosevelt's opponent was Alfred Landon, governor of Kansas. A former independent oil producer and conservative spender, Landon had managed to balance the budget in his state. Big money interests backing him hoped he would do the same for the nation. Landon attacked the New Deal for its waste

A farmer and his sons brave the dust storms rather than leave their home in Oklahoma during 1936. This photo was taken by Arthur Rothstein as part of the Farm Security Administration's program to record conditions.

of funds with few results. He also blamed Roosevelt for ignoring the Constitution and creating an out-of-control system of federal government.

It was not only Landon attacking the president and the New Deal. Phil La Follette, governor of Wisconsin, summed it up as the price Roosevelt had to pay for leadership. And the president was indeed a visible target since the entire New Deal appeared to be the actions of a single man. Despite "wasteful" New Deal agencies, there were signs of people being helped. In Colorado, cash income for farmers had nearly doubled. In Detroit, newly unionized workers were making better wages. And throughout the country, Social Security was operating.[2] Unemployment was down to 9 million (from 12 million)[3] and the stock market was up. The more things improved, though, the louder the anti-Roosevelt camp howled.

Roosevelt did not begin campaigning with enthusiasm until October 1936. As far as Roosevelt was concerned, the election hinged on a single issue: "The issue in this campaign is myself and people must be either for me or against me."[4] He pointed out how Landon changed his speeches to suit what the people wanted to hear rather than making promises he intended to keep. When Roosevelt said, "I don't make one speech in the East and another in the West," a reporter is said to have shouted out, "No, it's the same old bull everywhere."[5] In the East, Roosevelt was delighted to see subway riders wearing Roosevelt buttons, then switching to Landon buttons (to please the bosses) as the Wall Street station appeared. In the West, he was greeted with signs that read "Thank God for Roosevelt."[6] Among the crowds he heard people exclaim, "He saved my home" and "He gave me a job."[7] His campaign platform focused on pointing out all that his administration had accomplished. He reminded people what conditions were like before he took office and that he had yet to balance the budget.

More people showed up at the polls to vote in the 1936 election than had in 1932. The national average was 61 percent, but in some states voter turnout was even higher. In West Virginia, an astounding 84.9 percent of registered voters cast ballots.[8] Roosevelt won the election in a landslide. Landon only won the states of Maine and Vermont.[9] The forgotten man—laborers and skilled workers—continued to believe in the president's New Deal. Men like Mr. Donner (full name unavailable), who was working for the WPA after losing his printing business, patiently waited for the return of the lives they once knew. Roosevelt now had another four years to find a way to pull the nation from the tight grip of the Depression.

Natural Disasters

The country was plagued by natural disasters. Dust storms still ravaged the West—the Great Plains was now known as the Dust Bowl. Caroline A. Henderson, a farmer with her husband in Oklahoma for twenty-eight years, described their experience in the *Atlantic Monthly* in May 1936: "Wearing our shade hats, with handkerchiefs tied over our faces and Vaseline in our nostrils, we have been trying to rescue our home from the accumulation of wind-blown dust which penetrates wherever air can go. It is an almost hopeless task, for there is rarely a day when at some time the dust clouds do not roll over. 'Visibility' approaches zero and everything is covered again with a silt-like deposit which may vary in depth from a film to actual ripples on the kitchen floor."[10]

"Migrant Mother," taken by Dorothea Lange for the Farm Security Administration, is one of the most famous photographs from the Depression era. Taken in 1936, in Nipano, California, it shows a migrant pea picker distraught after news that freezing rain had damaged the crop.

A boat on a main street serves as means of transportation on flooded streets of Kentucky. Heavy rains after a series of tornadoes in 1936 caused the Ohio River to overflow its banks.

Tornadoes hit the South from Georgia into Kansas. From April 2 to 6, 1936, the second deadliest outbreak of tornadoes in United States history—seventeen separate twisters in all—hit five states.[11] The tornadoes killed 466 people, injured 3,457, and caused $25 million in damage.[12] What made this natural disaster especially crushing was that Tupelo, Mississippi, the first city to benefit from the power generated by the TVA, was devastated. Businesses left vacant due to the Great Depression were turned into instant morgues. The movie theater in Tupelo became a make-shift hospital and the popcorn machine was used to sterilize medical instruments.[13] Heavy rains from the tornadoes caused the Ohio, Mississippi, and

Allegheny rivers to rise. Floods caused damage—taking lives and destroying homes—from Indiana to Kentucky when those rivers overflowed.

"Court-Packing"

In addition to the turmoil of Mother Nature, the executive branch of the federal government was squabbling with the other two branches. After the Supreme Court denounced New Deal programs, Congress was tougher in passing new recovery plans. FDR tried to pass a new law to increase the number of Supreme Court justices so he could appoint justices sympathetic to his New Deal programs. This attempt was called "court-packing." Roosevelt hoped it would stop the Supreme Court's unfavorable decisions on the New Deal programs. Congress refused to help. The court-packing plan failed.

FDR's stubbornness regarding the court-packing both helped and hindered him. Two of the existing justices, possibly in response to the controversy, began voting to uphold New Deal achievements. In a sense, this created the effective liberal majority that FDR wanted. But the Democrats, who had always backed FDR in Congress, became divided. After his court-packing attempt, few important reforms were passed through Congress.[14]

Unionizing

While the battles going on in the branches of the federal government were not physically violent, labor

SOURCE DOCUMENT

THE COURT, IN ADDITION TO THE PROPER USE OF ITS JUDICIAL FUNCTION, HAS IMPROPERLY SET ITSELF UP AS A THIRD HOUSE OF CONGRESS—A SUPERLEGISLATURE, AS ONE OF THE JUSTICES HAS CALLED IT, "READING INTO THE CONSTITUTION WORDS AND IMPLICATIONS WHICH ARE NOT THERE AND WHICH WERE NEVER INTENDED TO BE THERE.

WE HAVE, THEREFORE, REACHED THE POINT AS A NATION WHERE WE MUST TAKE ACTION TO SAVE THE CONSTITUTION FROM THE COURT AND THE COURT FROM ITSELF. WE MUST FIND A WAY TO TAKE AN APPEAL FROM THE SUPREME COURT TO THE CONSTITUTION ITSELF. WE WANT A SUPREME COURT WHICH WILL DO JUSTICE UNDER THE CONSTITUTION—NOT OVER IT. IN OUR COURTS WE WANT A GOVERNMENT OF LAWS AND NOT OF MEN.

I WANT—AS ALL AMERICANS WANT—AN INDEPENDENT JUDICIARY AS PROPOSED BY THE FRAMERS OF THE CONSTITUTION. THAT MEANS A SUPREME COURT THAT WILL ENFORCE THE CONSTITUTION AS WRITTEN—THAT WILL REFUSE TO AMEND THE CONSTITUTION BY THE ARBITRARY EXERCISE OF JUDICIAL POWER, AMENDMENT BY JUDICIAL SAY-SO.[15]

President Roosevelt delivered a radio address on March 9, 1937, advocating his court-packing bill.

strikes—which were becoming widespread—were. Automobile workers organized the United Automobile Workers (UAW) of America in 1935. Workers in Flint, Michigan, began a sit-down strike on December 30, 1936, which lasted until March 12, 1937.

In a sit-down strike, workers refused to work on the assembly line or to leave the factory. If they stayed at their workstations, the company could not replace them with other workers. Women—some workers, some wives of workers—picketed outside the plants. The picketing was often used as a distraction while union organizers targeted another plant.

The UAW was a fledgling union, and for its first thirteen days, the strike at General Motors' Fisher body plant in Flint was peaceful but tense. On January 11, 1937, the tension escalated into an armed clash. Frustrated with the peaceful "sit-down" and realizing the strike could seriously stall production, managers summoned the Flint police. Determined to drive the strikers out, the officers arrived in riot gear. They broke windows, firing tear-gas grenades and buckshot into the plant. The strikers retaliated by throwing whatever was at hand. Bricks, steel hinges, and bottles showered down on the officers. For the next month, the strikers held their ground—and the Flint plant.[16]

The strike spread from Flint to the rest of General Motors' fourteen-state empire. Facing losses of a million dollars a day, General Motors caved in on February 11. They signed a contract giving the UAW unprecedented bargaining power. Other automakers— and major industries nationwide—were sure to follow. "Even if we got not one . . . thing out of it other than that," recalled one striker, "we at least had a right to open our mouths without fear."[17]

The strike officially ended on March 12, 1937. General Motors agreed to recognize the UAW as the bargaining agent for workers. The success of the UAW inspired others as unions grew across the nation. The sit-down strike was more effective than a picket line when unions were new. It forced management to address the issues rather than dismissing the unions and the unionized workers.[18]

Strike fever swept the country as workers rushed to join what *Fortune* magazine called "one of the greatest mass movements in our history."[19] That movement was, at times, a bloody endeavor. In May 1937, the UAW targeted Ford Motor's River Rouge plant in Michigan. While union organizers handed out pamphlets, violence erupted. Eighteen people, including four women, were hurt. A month later, Chicago police used gunfire to break up a rally of fifteen hundred Republic Steel employees and their families, killing ten and wounding more than one hundred. In industry after industry, the struggles of 1937 shifted the balance of power between employer and employee. Unions became a political, social, and economic force that changed the fortunes of the individual worker and the nation itself.[20]

Recession

Progress made in recovering from the Depression was set back by a recession. A recession is a downward slump in the economy after a period of steady growth. The decade-long Great Depression would have been a difficult experience under any conditions. Its blow was more crushing because it struck the high-spirited, happy population enjoying the dramatic economic growth following World War I. Americans had assumed those merry times were the norm.

Americans now feared that not even FDR, the man they had poured all their hope into supporting, could pull the country from the depths of the Depression. In 1937, Robert and Helen Lynd described the recession's impact on an Indiana town:

> The city had been shaken for nearly six years by a catastrophe involving not only people's values but, in the case of many, their very existence. Unlike most socially generated catastrophes, in this case virtually nobody in the community had been cushioned against the blow; the great knife of the depression had cut down impartially through the entire population, cleaving open the lives and hopes of rich as well as poor. The experience had been more nearly universal than any prolonged recent emotional experience in the city's history; it had approached in its elemental shock the primary experiences of birth and death.[21]

Opponents to FDR and the New Deal blamed the slump on the president's spending to create jobs, referring to this crisis as "FDR's recession." The economic slump was in part from a premature effort by the administration to balance the budget. Farm prices dropped drastically. In an effort to help raise the prices, farmers tried to stop deliveries of dairy products and crops in near riotlike encounters with truck drivers. During 1937, unemployment doubled, reaching 11 million by May 1938. Faced with record unemployment and hoping to increase mass purchasing power, FDR abandoned efforts to balance the budget. Instead he started a $5 billion spending program in the spring of 1938.[22]

FDR made one final effort to boost the economy and end the recession. It was the last major domestic achievement of the Roosevelt administration. The Fair Labor Standards Act, passed in 1938, established a national minimum wage and set limits on hours of work. By the end of the year, the New Deal had effectively come to an end.[23] What more could his administration do? The nation put the recession behind it but still the Depression lingered.

11

DISCORD WITHOUT

This nation will remain a neutral nation . . . I have seen war and . . . I hate war . . . I hope the United States will keep out of this war. I believe that it will.[1]

—President Franklin D. Roosevelt, fireside chat, 1939

In addition to troubles in the United States, Europe was also undergoing a depression and major policy changes. FDR's attention was drawn to the turmoil in Europe, since Congress strongly opposed further domestic reforms. When war erupted in Europe in 1939, FDR was determined to keep the United States out of it.

Roosevelt was concerned over world affairs because nations were taking over other countries without any resistance. The Axis powers (Germany, Italy, and Japan) seized control of neighboring countries. At the Munich Conference in 1938, Hitler promised leaders of Great Britain and France that a small section of Czechoslovakia was the last territory he was after. In March 1939, he broke his promise and invaded the rest of Czechoslovakia. Italy and Japan made similar moves against their neighbors. The Axis powers did this unchecked by other nations.

War Abroad

Adolf Hitler became chancellor of Germany, or head of state, in 1933—the same year President Roosevelt entered his first term as president. During the time dust storms raged across the midwestern United States, fascism (government headed by a dictator in which all religious, social, political, and economic programs are strictly controlled) and communism were storming across Europe and Asia. Germany, Italy, and Japan were three nations the American people and the Roosevelt administration had kept one eye on while devising ways to maintain American democracy and fight the worldwide depression.

As those three countries swept up their neighbors through military conquest, the American people were fearful about fighting in another war. Through fireside chats, FDR assured the people he planned to remain out of the war. Disillusioned with the outcome of World War I, the American people clung to isolationism (a policy where a country looks after its own interests and does not join in alliances with other countries). Most felt it had been a mistake to enter World War I, and they wanted the United States to stay out of conflicts overseas. While the United States was strongly detached from the conflicts abroad, FDR noted that France and Great Britain were too busy pulling their countries out of the worldwide depression to interfere with invasions of territory in Europe. FDR kept watch on Benito

Students at the University of California at Berkeley wanted the United States to remain out of the war in Europe. The gathering crowd was so large it flowed out Sather Gate.

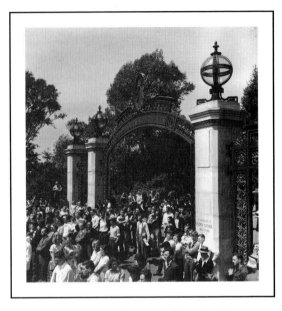

Mussolini, leader of Italy, Hitler, and the Japanese rulers. Japan stormed through China while Mussolini invaded Africa and Hitler remilitarized the Rhineland and captured surrounding countries.

Price of Neutrality

The United States remained neutral through the provisions of the Neutrality Act. It was actually one of three related laws. The first Neutrality Act, passed in 1935, prohibited the United States from furnishing weapons or supplies to any nation at war. The Neutrality Act was amended in 1937 to prohibit granting loans to warring countries and also extended to civil wars. In 1939, the act was revised to allow American manufacturers to supply warring nations on a "cash-and-carry" basis. The nation offered to help countries involved in strife—Spain, for example, was involved in a civil war—by selling them weapons and planes. They had to pay in cash and provide their own

SOURCE DOCUMENT

EXPORT OF ARMS, AMMUNITION, AND IMPLEMENTS OF WAR

SECTION 1. (A) WHENEVER THE PRESIDENT SHALL FIND THAT THERE EXISTS A STATE OF WAR BETWEEN, OR AMONG, TWO OR MORE FOREIGN STATES, THE PRESIDENT SHALL PROCLAIM SUCH FACT, AND IT SHALL THEREAFTER BE UNLAWFUL TO EXPORT, OR ATTEMPT TO EXPORT, OR CAUSE TO BE EXPORTED, ARMS, AMMUNITION, OR IMPLEMENTS OF WAR FROM ANY PLACE IN THE UNITED STATES TO ANY BELLIGERENT STATE NAMED IN SUCH PROCLAMATION, OR TO ANY NEUTRAL STATE FOR TRANSSHIPMENT TO, OR FOR THE USE OF, ANY SUCH BELLIGERENT STATE.[2]

The Neutrality Act of 1937 was signed into law on May 1.

ships to transport the supplies. The law spelled out the United States position as a country intending to remain objective about political strife abroad. By refusing to trade or barter materials and supplies used for war, or to sell on credit, the United States felt they were clearly making the point that this was a non-American war and the government refused any involvement.

As early as 1933, news of the hateful treatment of Jews and others considered inferior by the Nazis reached the United States.[3] Like fascism, Nazism tightly diminished personal freedom but permitted private ownership of property. The Nazis glorified fair-haired, blue-eyed Germans and other similar-looking northern Europeans. They called these types of people the Aryan

As Nazism grew in Germany at the end of the 1930s, personal freedoms in that country declined. Here, thousands of books expressing ideas contrary to Nazi views smolder in a huge bonfire as Germans give Nazi salute.

race and claimed they were superior. They claimed that Jews, Slavs, and other minorities were inferior. Jews had to register with the government. Their personal property and many privileges were taken away. Many Americans claimed sympathy for the victims of the Nazi rule. Still, they did not want the United States involved in the fight. Nazism also strongly opposed any government or movement that affirmed equality. Nazi plans to create a harmonious and prosperous German state resulted in terrorism, mass murder, and the advent of World War II.

World War II was underway with the Nazi invasion of Poland in 1939. American isolationist sentiment intensified. The Roosevelt administration turned its attention from domestic affairs to focus on international strife. Efforts to allow refugees into the United States failed. In Congress, proposals to adjust the immigration quota (number of people allowed into the country during a certain time period) were defeated. A 1938 opinion poll by *Fortune* magazine found less than 5 percent of Americans agreeable to raising immigration quotas. The other 95 percent claimed that with current conditions due to the Depression, it was best "to keep them [refugees] out."[4] More Jewish refugees fled Nazi rule. Between 1940 and 1941, rumors of concentration camps reached the United States.[5] At first, the camps were reported to house opponents to Nazism and other criminals. Soon, all Jews were rounded up and sent to the camps as forced labor. FDR's hands were tied because of the Neutrality Act. He could only wait until public opinion changed or events altered America's need for involvement.

Day of Infamy

In less than a year, the binds of isolationism were severed. Early on Sunday morning, December 7, 1941, the Japanese attacked Pearl Harbor, an American naval base in Hawaii. The first wave of the attack came quickly. It was 7:58 A.M. The factor of surprise was jolting to the men who had moments before started their Sunday morning routines. Wave after wave of torpedo and dive

The Japanese attack on the American naval base in Pearl Harbor, Hawaii, on December 7, 1941, was quick and fierce. Here the USS Arizona *burns in the harbor.*

bombers swooped down on the navy fleet in Pearl Harbor. As quickly as they had appeared, the enemy bombers withdrew to their aircraft carriers stationed about three hundred miles away. The attack ended at 9:45 A.M. Within two hours, the United States Navy suffered heavy casualties—2,000 men killed and 710 wounded. The army and marines reported 327 dead and 433 wounded. In addition, 70 civilians were killed.[6]

The United States retaliated. President Roosevelt called the attack "a date which will live in infamy,"[7] and asked Congress to declare war on Japan on Monday,

December 8, 1941. Congress quickly complied, confirming the president's declaration only six-and-a-half minutes later.[8]

In keeping with their agreements in the Tripartite Pact, an Axis agreement of alliance, Germany and Italy then declared war upon the United States. America, about as prepared for World War II as it had been prepared for the Great Depression, was embarking on a new and uneasy journey.

Unifying the War Effort

American industry geared up to produce tanks, aircraft, and other war items. The Selective Service Act of 1940 required all men ages 21 to 35 to register for one year of military service. The first soldier drafted under this act entered the army on November 18, 1940. Amendments to the act extended the age from 18 to 44 and required service for the duration of the war. Due to the draft, the CCC disbanded by 1942. Many young CCC men had already learned how to take orders, in addition to other boot camp skills directly transferable in time of war. The spirit of both men and women was fired up. Millions joined the armed forces to fight for victory at home and abroad. As men left for the front lines, women become the industrial producers of military equipment.

With most men gone to the front, many women lived, worked, and traveled alone for the first time in their lives. They were also called upon to do jobs previously thought unsuitable for women, such as

While men were battling on the front line in Europe, women worked on the home front. Women took on jobs normally reserved for men, such as chipping and welding.

welding. Traditional expectations were cast aside as women joined unions and donned military uniforms—as members of the Women's Army Corps (WAC), assigned to the Army Air Forces or other female military organizations. "It really opened up another viewpoint on life," a female aircraft worker recalled.[9]

Families across the country moved from struggling to make ends meet to willingly sacrificing. Rationing, or reserving, supplies such as gas, rubber, and food became the norm. The sacrifice was made willingly "for the good of the country" and the war cause. With the boom in manufacturing supplies and weapons for war, the economy improved. It took the mass production of World War II for the United States to finally leave the Great Depression behind.

12

MOVING FORWARD

We are not going to turn the clock back! We are going forward my friends . . . We are going forward together.[1]

—Franklin D. Roosevelt

FDR's New Deal did not end the Depression, though it brought some relief to morale and eased much of the country's economic distress. It took the onset of World War II, however, to turn the economy around. About 8 million Americans still had no jobs in 1940. Military spending for World War II created both the jobs and the economic growth needed to bring back prosperity. And it created the confidence and buoyant spirit America needed. "A Depression is much like a run on a bank. It's a crisis of confidence," Raymond Moley, former Brain Trust advisor to FDR, told broadcaster and author Studs Terkel in a 1970 interview. "The bank rescue of 1933 was probably the turning point of the Depression. . . . Most of the legislation that came after didn't really help the public. The public helped itself, after it got confidence."[2]

If the New Deal is an example of faltering notions and poor economic planning, it is a shining example of creating needed change. The New Deal did not bring about the utopia many hoped it would. It did not dramatically redistribute wealth. It did not address racial or social shames of the past. Instead, its success lies in the significant change it created in the role of the federal government. To step in and manage the affairs of the nation required cooperation among all aspects and levels of society. The reforms created by the New Deal endured throughout World War II. Many are still in effect today—from Social Security and accessible home mortgages to cheap electricity and a supervised stock market.

Women factory workers put finishing touches on the transparent noses for deadly A-20 attack bombers at the Douglas Aircraft plant in Long Beach, California.

A New Government

Between 1933 and 1939, Roosevelt's administration created twenty-one federal programs and agencies to fight economic depression. These new organizations permanently expanded the roles of the federal government in American life. American people, whether laborers or politicians, can now lobby the government to meet their economic and social needs. Prior to the New Deal, such influence was reserved for business interests. The New Deal also produced a new political alliance that supported the Democrats as the majority party in national politics for more than a generation after it ended.[3]

Most scholars agree that the New Deal saved the basics of the American free-enterprise system. Profits and competition continued to play a leading role. The added feature was the federal government assuming responsibility for the economic security of the people and the economic growth of the nation. Prior to the New Deal this was unheard of. Such government responsibility bordered on interference. During the Depression it became necessary. The federal government's role in public welfare continues to this day.

Legacy of the New Deal

Most programs were federally funded work programs. The driving force behind them was that Americans needed to feel wanted and be productive. These programs helped ensure the continuance of the American free-enterprise system we know today.

Many New Deal laws and policies also remain with us. Today's standard workweek is now five days instead of six. Workers have the right to unionize and can depend upon compensation when they are laid off or unemployed. Social Security provides some compensation for retirement.

The Public Works Administration (PWA) focused on large-scale construction of roads, bridges, dams, public housing projects, and public buildings such as hospitals, college dormitories, and post offices. Most are in use today. The Federal Art Project, part of the Work Projects Administration (WPA), hired artists to paint murals inside some of these buildings. The Federal Art Project also hired musicians and actors to perform around the country. Many Americans saw live performances for the first time. Writers were employed to record local history as part of the Federal Writer's Program. The Federal Art Project awakened a cultural change in the United States. Access to the arts—music, books, dance, plays, and museums—is something many Americans, not only the upper class, pursue as a pastime.

The WPA hired men who were sole wage earners for their families. They built roads, bridges, parks, public swimming pools, airport runways, small dams, and roadside drainage. By the time the program ended in 1943, the WPA had employed 8.5 million workers.[4] "Whenever we traveled one of those roads or saw one of those dams, I was proud to be able to tell my children and grandchildren, 'I helped build that,'" said Basil McGuire of Ocala, Florida.[5]

One of the greatest legacies of the New Deal is the conservation efforts of the Civilian Conservation Corps (CCC). Americans today still use and enjoy the camps, forests, and parks young CCC workers helped build and beautify. Accomplishments of the CCC are among the most outstanding of all New Deal agencies. The first national effort to restore the country's natural resources, the CCC employed over 3 million men who planted 2.3 billion trees and spent a great amount of time fighting forest fires and eradicating diseases and pests on 21 million acres of land.[6]

"The discipline and self-respect that I gained in the CCC was invaluable. It smoothed the way for my Navy service in World War II, and it helped me appreciate life in general. I wouldn't trade my experiences for anything," said Joseph Lee of Porter, Indiana.[7]

As Moley said, the Depression was a crisis of confidence. The results of the programs created by the New Deal provided renewed personal confidence for the American people. It also created an entirely new confidence for the American people in their federal government. While young and old alike gained discipline and maintained self-respect, the federal government gained a sense of responsibility. Through laws regulating banking as well as business-labor dealings, that responsibility remains in place today.

★ TIMELINE ★

1929—*October:* Stock market crashes; Wall Street in panic; economy declines rapidly.

1930—Unemployment increases; President Hoover reluctant to act.

1932—*July:* Federal troops clear capital of "Bonus Army," World War I veterans seeking early payout of military bonus.

November 8: Franklin Delano Roosevelt elected thirty-second president of the United States; Refuses to work with Hoover administration, wishing for a fresh start when his own administration takes over.

1933—*January through March:* Public panic escalates as economy declines and banks close doors; Estimated 15 million workers, or one in four, unemployed.

March 4: Roosevelt's inauguration.

March 5–June 16: Congress enacts New Deal recovery measures including banking holiday, FDIC, Truth-in-Securities Act, and establishes Agricultural Adjustment Administration and National Recovery Administration during what came to be known as the "First One Hundred Days."

March 12: President Roosevelt gives first of his famous "fireside" chats broadcast over national radio.

December 5: Prohibition repealed.

1934—Drought and dust storms across the Great Plains destroy crops and livestock; Country sees first drop in unemployment since stock market crash; Federal Communications Commission founded to regulate radio, telephone, and telegraph systems; Radio priest Charles E. Coughlin, who supported FDR during election, now criticizes New Deal policies.

April: Civil Works Administration is terminated.

June 6: Securities and Exchange Commission founded to regulate sales of securities and ensure fair stock market practices.

1935—*March:* Works Progress Administration founded.

May: Supreme Court declares National Recovery Act unconstitutional; Section 7 allowing for unionization of labor is retained.

August: The Social Security Act and the first Neutrality Act are passed; National Youth Administration is founded to provide job training for unemployed youths and part-time work for needy students.

1936—*January 6:* Supreme Court declares Agricultural Adjustment Act unconstitutional.

November 3: Roosevelt wins reelection.

1937—*February 1:* Floods hit Midwest; WPA workers try to stop flood waters with sandbag walls.

July: Supreme Court controversy begins when Roosevelt tries "court-packing," or trying to increase the number of Supreme Court justices so he could appoint justices who favored his recovery programs.

1938—*June 25:* Minimum-wage law set.

1939—*January 30:* Supreme Court upholds Tennessee Valley Authority as constitutional.

September 4: United States remains neutral as war erupts in Europe.

November 4: The United States agrees to sell arms to friendly countries on a "cash-and-carry" basis.

1940—Roosevelt wins reelection; Selective Service Act is passed by Congress to draft young men into armed service.

1941—The Atlantic Charter is issued.

December: Japan attacks Pearl Harbor; United States declares war.

United States economy gears up to supply armed forces with war equipment and materials.

★ Chapter Notes ★

Chapter 1. The Forgotten Man

1. Stephen Donadio, et al, ed., *The New York Public Library Book of Twentieth-Century American Quotations* (New York: Stonesong Press, 1992), p. 381.

2. David A. Shannon, *The Great Depression* (Englewood Cliffs, N.J.: Prentice-Hall, Inc. 1960), p. 147.

3. Ibid., p. 148.

4. David F. Burg, *The Great Depression: An Eyewitness History* (New York: Facts on File, Inc., 1996), p. 168.

5. T. H. Watkins, *The Great Depression: America in the 1930s* (New York: Blackside, Inc., 1993), pp. 258–259.

6. Robert S. McElvaine, ed., *Down & Out in the Great Depression* (Chapel Hill: University of North Carolina Press, 1983), pp. 145–154.

7. Shannon, p. 149.

8. Ibid., p. 150.

9. Ibid.

Chapter 2. Shattered Prosperity

1. David Colbert, ed., *Eyewitness to America* (New York: Pantheon Books, 1997), p. 370.

2. Vincent Virga and Alan Brinkley, *Eyes of the Nation: A Visual History of the United States* (New York: Alfred A. Knopf, 1997), p. 257.

3. Ibid., p. 258.

4. Ibid., p. 257.

5. Sarah Brash and Loretta Britten, ed., *Events that Shaped the Century* (New York: Time-Life Books, 1998), p. 78.

6. Studs Terkel, *Hard Times: An Oral History of the Great Depression* (New York: Pantheon, 1970), pp. 65–66.

7. Fon Wyman Boardman, *America and the Jazz Age: A History of the 1920's* (New York: Henry Z. Walck, Inc., 1968), p. 118.

8. Brash and Britten, p. 78.

9. Elliott V. Bell, *Eyewitness to America,* ed. by David Colbert (New York: Pantheon Books, 1997), p. 371.

10. Ibid.

11. Ibid.

12. Ibid., p. 369.

13. Ibid., p. 370.

14. Ibid., p. 369.

15. Ibid.

16. Deb Mulvey, ed., *We Had Everything But Money* (Greendale, Wis.: Reiman Publications, 1992), p. 10.

17. T. H. Watkins, *The Hungry Years: A Narrative History of the Great Depression in America* (New York: Henry Holt, 1999), p. 40.

18. *Historical Statistics of the United States* (Washington, D.C.: U.S. Department of Commerce, U.S. Government Printing Office, 1975), p. 126.

19. Roger Biles, *A New Deal for the American People* (DeKalb: Northern Illinois University Press, 1991), p. 14.

20. Ibid., p. 15.

Chapter 3. Down and Out

1. Stephen Donadio, et al, ed., *The New York Public Library Book of Twentieth-Century American Quotations* (New York: Stonesong Press, 1992), p. 149.

2. Sarah Brash and Loretta Britten, ed., *Events that Shaped the Century* (New York: Time-Life Books, 1998), p. 82.

3. Studs Terkel, *Hard Times: An Oral History of the Great Depression* (New York: Pantheon, 1970), p. 275.

4. Marc McCutcheon, *The Writer's Guide to Everyday Life from Prohibition through World War II* (Cincinnati: Writer's Digest Books, 1995), pp. 68–70.

5. Lewis Lord, "1933: The Rise of the Common Man," *U.S. News & World Report,* October 25, 1993, p. 10.

6. Ibid.

7. Roger Biles, *A New Deal for the American People* (DeKalb: Northern Illinois University Press, 1991), p. 24.

8. Brash and Britten, p. 82.

9. Robert S. McElvaine, *The Depression and New Deal* (New York: Oxford University Press, 2000), p. 20.

10. David Colbert, ed., *Eyewitness to America* (New York: Pantheon Books, 1997), p. 377.

11. Ibid., pp. 375–378.

12. Biles, p. 25.

13. T. H. Watkins, *The Hungry Years: A Narrative History of the Great Depression in America* (New York: Henry Holt, 1999), p. 140.

Chapter 4. Campaigning a New Deal

1. James A. Haggerty, "Roosevelt Hailed by 15,000 in Boston," *The New York Times,* November 1, 1931, p. 16.

2. Roger Biles, *A New Deal for the American People* (DeKalb: Northern Illinois University Press, 1991), p. 11.

3. Ibid.

4. Ibid.

5. Ibid., p. 25.

6. Ibid.

7. "Roosevelt's Nomination Address, Chicago, Ill., July 2, 1932," *Works of Franklin D. Roosevelt*, n.d., <http://newdeal.feri.org/speeches/1932b.htm> (November 29, 2001).

8. Biles, p. 26.

9. "Three-Point Program Advocated by Gov. Roosevelt for Meeting Immediate Problem of Unemployment," *The New York Times,* Tuesday, November 1, 1932, p. 1.

10. Biles, p. 29.

11. Ibid.

12. Ibid., p. 30.

13. Larry Madanas and James M. SoRelle, ed., *Taking Sides: Clashing Views on Controversial Issues in American History, Vol. II, Reconstruction to the Present,* sixth ed. (Guilford, Conn.: Dushlein Publishing Group, 1995), p. 237.

14. Biles, p. 31.

15. "Franklin D. Roosevelt, First Inaugural Address, March 4, 1933," January 20, 1996, <http://douglass. speech.nwu.edu/roos_a76.htm> (November 29, 2001).

16. Ibid.

Chapter 5. The Great Communicator

1. "Fourth Inaugural Address of Franklin D. Roosevelt," *The Avalon Project at the Yale Law School,* November 29, 2001, <http://www.yale.edu/lawweb/avalon/presiden/inaug/froos4. htm> (November 29, 2001).

2. Ted Morgan, *FDR* (New York: Simon & Schuster, 1985), pp. 26–27.

3. Ibid., p. 19.

4. Studs Terkel, *Hard Times: An Oral History of the Great Depression* (New York: Pantheon, 1970), pp. 262–265.

5. James A. Haggerty, "Roosevelt Hailed by 15,000 in Boston," *The New York Times,* November 1, 1932, sec. 1, p. 16.

6. James A. Farley, "Executive Has Free Hand," *The New York Times,* November 10, 1932, p. 4.

7. "Franklin D. Roosevelt, First Inaugural Address, March 4, 1933," January 20, 1996, <http://douglass. speech.nwu.edu/roos_a76.htm> (November 29, 2001).

8. Robert S. McElvaine, *The Depression and New Deal: A History in Documents* (New York: Oxford University Press, 2000), pp. 48–51.

9. Lewis Lord, "1933: The Rise of the Common Man," *U.S. News & World Report,* October 25, 1993, p. 10.

10. David Colbert, ed., *Eyewitness to America* (New York: Pantheon Books, 1997), p. 379.

11. Vincent Virga and Alan Brinkley, *Eyes of the Nation: A Visual History of the United States* (New York: Alfred A. Knopf, 1997), p. 265.

Chapter 6. The First One Hundred Days

1. James A. Haggerty, "Roosevelt Hailed by 15,000 in Boston," *The New York Times,* November 1, 1932, sec. 1, p. 16.

2. David F. Burg, *The Great Depression: An Eyewitness History* (New York: Facts on File, Inc., 1996), p. 107.

3. Lois and Alan Gordon, *American Chronicle: Six Decades in American Life 1920–1980* (New York: Atheneum, 1987), pp. 127–145.

4. Burg, pp. 106–108.

5. Sarah Brash and Loretta Britten, ed., *Events that Shaped the Century* (New York: Time-Life Books, 1998), p. 86.

6. Burg, pp. 111–114.

7. Alan Brinkley, "A New Deal for America," *Social Education*, September 1996, p. 257; Burg, pp. 117–119.

8. Burg, p. 318.

9. Patrick J. Maney "FDR: The Illusive Standard," *Prologue*, NARA Spring 1994, pp. 32–47.

10. Larry Madanas and James M. SoRelle, ed., *Taking Sides: Clashing Views on Controversial Issues in American History, Vol. II, Reconstruction to the Present,* sixth ed. (Guilford, Conn.: Dushlein Publishing Group, 1995), p. 237.

11. Maney, pp. 32–47.

12. Lewis Lord, "1933: The Rise of the Common Man," *U.S. News & World Report,* October 25, 1993, p. 10.

13. Brash and Britten, p. 86.

Chapter 7. ABCs of Reform

1. "The President for Life," *Franklin Delano Roosevelt*, n.d., <http://www.americanpresident.org/Kotrain/courses/FDR/FDR_Domestic_Affairs.htm> (April 26, 2002).

2. David F. Burg, *The Great Depression: An Eyewitness History* (New York: Facts on File, Inc., 1996), p. 108.

3. David Colbert, ed., *Eyewitness to America* (New York: Pantheon Books, 1997), p. 381.

19. Ibid., p. 228.

20. Bennett, p. 121.

21. Michael E. Parrish, *Anxious Decades: America in Prosperity and Depression, 1920–1941* (New York: Norton, 1992), p. 337.

22. Burg, p. 147.

Chapter 9. The Second One Hundred Days

1. Arthur Schlesinger, Jr., "The Real Roosevelt Legacy," *Newsweek,* October 14, 1996, p. 43.

2. Robert S. McElvaine, ed., *Down & Out in the Great Depression* (Chapel Hill: University of North Carolina Press, 1983), p. 208.

3. Alan Brinkley, "A New Deal for America," *Social Education*, September 1996, p. 257.

4. David F. Burg, *The Great Depression: An Eyewitness History* (New York: Facts on File, Inc., 1996), p. 151.

5. Lois and Alan Gordon, *American Chronicle: Six Decades in American Life 1920–1980* (New York: Atheneum, 1987), pp. 97–98.

6. Milton Meltzer, *Violins and Shovels: The WPA Arts Projects* (New York: Delacorte Press, 1976), p. 116.

7. Michael J. Sandel, "Anti-Social Security," *New Republic,* February 3, 1997, vol. 216, no. 5, p. 27.

8. "Social Security Act, Title 1," n.d. <http://www.ssa.gov/OP_Home/ssact/title00/0000.htm> (November 29, 2001).

9. Frances Perkins, "Social Insurance for U.S.," February 25, 1935, <http://www.ssa.gov/history/perkinsradio.html> (November 29, 2001).

10. Sandel, p. 27

11. T. H. Watkins, *The Hungry Years: A Narrative History of the Great Depression in America* (New York: Henry Holt and Co., 1999), pp. 442–443.

12. "An Eyewitness Account," *Surviving the Dust Bowl*, n.d. <http://www.pbs.org/wgbh/amex/dustbowl/sfeature/eyewitness.html> (November 29, 2001).

13. Sarah Brash and Loretta Britten, ed., *Events that Shaped the Century* (New York: Time-Life Books, 1998), p. 88.

14. Watkins, pp. 442–443.

Chapter 10. Discord Within

1. Franklin D. Roosevelt, Democratic National Convention speech, June 1936, *The New York Public Library Book of Twentieth-Century American Quotations* (New York: Stonesong Press, 1992), p. 109.

2. Ted Morgan, *FDR* (New York: Simon & Schuster, 1985), p. 428.

3. "Labor Force and Its Components: 1900 to 1947," *Historical Statistics of the United States: Colonial Times to 1970* (Washington, D.C.: U.S. Dept. of Commerce, U.S. Government Printing Office, 1975), p. 126.

4. Morgan, p. 429.

5. Ibid., p. 440.

6. Ibid.

7. Ibid.

8. T. H. Watkins, *The Hungry Years: A Narrative History of the Great Depression in America* (New York: Henry Holt and Co., 1999), p. 320.

9. Clifton Daniel, ed., *Chronicle of America* (Mount Kisco, N.Y.: Chronicle Publications/Prentice Hall, 1989), p. 673.

10. David F. Burg, *The Great Depression: An Eyewitness History* (New York: Facts on File, Inc., 1996), p. 178.

11. Benjamin A. Watson, *Acts of God: The Old Farmer's Almanac: Unpredictable Guide to Weather and Natural Disasters* (New York: Random House, 1993), p. 56.

12. Tracy Irons-Georges, ed., *Natural Disasters* (Pasadena, Calif.: Salem Press, 2000), p. 797.

13. Ibid.

14. Alan Brinkley, "A New Deal for America," *Social Education*, September 1996, p. 257.

15. "President Franklin D. Roosevelt's 'Fireside Chat,' March 9, 1937," n.d., <http://www.wku.edu/Government/ yfdrchat.htm> (November 29, 2001).

16. Sarah Brash and Loretta Britten, ed., *Events that Shaped the Century* (New York: Time-Life Books, 1998), p. 92.

17. Ibid.

18. "Labor Unions Rise," *The Depression News: The 1930s,* October 11, 2001, <http://www.sos.state.mi.us/history/ museum/explore/museums/hismus/1900-75/depressn/laborun. html> (November 29, 2001).

19. Brash and Britten, p. 92.

20. Daniel, p. 677.

21. Vincent Virga and Alan Brinkley, *Eyes of the Nation: A Visual History of the United States* (New York: Alfred A. Knopf, 1997), p. 264.

22. Brinkley, p. 258.

23. Ibid.

Chapter 11. Discord Without

1. Russell D. Buhite and David W. Levy, ed., *FDR's Fireside Chats* (Norman: University of Oklahoma Press, 1992), p. 151.

2. "The Neutrality Act, May 1, 1937," *U.S. Historical Documents Archive,* February 19, 1999, <w3.one.net/ ~mweiler/ushda/neut1937.htm> (November 29, 2001).

3. David M. Kennedy, *Freedom From Fear: The American People in Depression and War, 1929–1945* (New York: Oxford University Press, 1999), pp. 410–412.

4. Ibid., p. 415.

5. Ted Morgan, *FDR* (New York: Simon & Schuster, 1985), p. 507ff; "Henry Morgenthau, Jr." in *Biographical Encyclopedia of 20ᵗʰ-Century World Leaders,* John Powell, ed. (New York: Marshall Cavendish Corp, 2000), p. 1092.

6. Clifton Daniel, ed., *Chronicle of America* (Mount Kisco, N.Y.: Chronicle Publications/Prentice Hall, 1989), p. 698.

7. "Franklin D. Roosevelt's Pearl Harbor Speech," n.d., <http://bcn.boulder.co.us/government/national/speeches/spch2.html> (November 29, 2001).

8. Daniel, p. 699.

9. Vincent Virga and Alan Brinkley, *Eyes of the Nation: A Visual History of the United States* (New York: Alfred A. Knopf, 1997), p. 270.

Chapter 12. Moving Forward

1. "Campaign Address at Soldiers' Field, Chicago, Illinois," October 28, 1944, *Franklin Delano Roosevelt: President of the Century* <http://www.feri.org/fdr/speech01.htm> (November 29, 2001).

2. Studs Terkel, *Hard Times: An Oral History of the Great Depression* (New York: Pantheon Books, 1970), pp. 250–251.

3. Teresa O'Neill, ed., *The Great Depression: Opposing Viewpoints* (San Diego, Calif.: Greenhaven Press, 1994), p. 273.

4. Lois and Alan Gordon, *American Chronicle: Six Decades in American Life 1920–1980* (New York: Atheneum, 1987), pp. 97–98.

5. Deb Mulvey, ed., "Six Months in CCC Provided Lifetime of Pride in Work," *We Had Everything But Money: Priceless Memories of the Great Depression* (Greendale, Wis.: Reiman Publications, 1992), p. 56.

6. Roger L. Rosentreter, "Roosevelt's Tree Army, Michigan's Civilian Conservation Corps," February 5, 2001, <http://www.sos.state.mi.us/history/museum/techstuff/depressn/treearmy.html> (November 29, 2001).

7. Mulvey, p. 59.

★ FURTHER READING ★

Books

Brennan, Kristine. *The Stock Market Crash of 1929*. Philadelphia, Pa.: Chelsea House Publishers, 2000.

Farrell, Jacqueline. *The Great Depression*. San Diego, Calif.: Lucent Books, 1996.

Joseph, Paul. *Franklin D. Roosevelt*. Minneapolis: ABDO Publishing Company, 2000.

McArthur, Debra. *The Dust Bowl and the Depression In American History*. Berkeley Heights, N.J.: Enslow Publishers, Inc., 2002.

Sherrow, Victoria. *Hardship and Hope: America and the Great Depression*. New York: Twenty-first Century Books, 1997.

Stewart, Gail B. *The New Deal*. New York: New Discovery Books, 1993.

Internet Addresses

Library of Congress. "American Life Histories: Manuscripts from the Federal Writers' Project, 1936–1940." *American Memory Collection*. October 19, 1998. <http://memory.loc.gov/ammem/wpaintro/wpahome.html>.

Library of Congress. "The New Deal Stage: Selections from the Federal Theater Project, 1935–1939." *American Memory Collection*. September 23, 1999. <http://memory.loc.gov/ammem/fedtp/fthome.html>.

"New Deal Network." January 17, 2002. <http://newdeal.feri.org/index.htm>.

Magazines

Gordon, Myles. "The Fight for Welfare Rights," *Scholastic Update,* March 11, 1994, vol. 126, no. 11, p. 12.

McCollum, Sean. "Conquering Fear Itself," *Scholastic Update*, February 21, 1997, vol. 129, no. 10, p. 18.

★ INDEX ★